· PLANNING AND PLANTING WATER GARDENS ·

Water Gardens

PHILIP SWINDELLS

WARD LOCK

A Ward Lock Book

First published in the UK 1994

This edition published 1996
by Ward Lock
Wellington House, 125 Strand
LONDON WC2R 0BB

A Cassell Imprint

Distributed in the United States
by Sterling Publishing Co., Inc.
387 Park Avenue South, New York,
NY 10016-8810

Distributed in Australia
by Capricorn Link (Australia) Pty Ltd
2/13 Carrington Road, Castle Hill NSW 2154

A British Library Cataloguing in Publication Data
block for this book may be obtained from the
British Library

ISBN 0-7063-7491-6

Text filmset by Litho Link Ltd, Welshpool, Powys, Wales.
Printed and bound in Singapore by Craft Print Pte Ltd.

Previous page: Moving water can be naturally achieved by
creating a waterfall. Modern pumps make
this safe and simple.

Contents

Preface 5

Acknowledgements 6

1 · Creating a Water Garden 7

2 · Constructing a Water Garden 22

3 · Moving Water 42

4 · Plants and Planting 58

5 · Fish and Other Livestock 74

6 · Managing the Water Garden 82

7 · The Water Gardener's Calendar 89

Appendix: Selected Water Garden Specialists ... 92

Index 94

◄ A water garden with all
the ingredients for success.
The planting is well
balanced and easy
to manage.

Preface

For centuries man has had a love affair with water. In the garden this can manifest itself in great beauty and ingenuity, for not only is water a medium for growing plants, but an element of beauty which can be used to great effect. The introduction of water provides endless opportunities for the artist and the keen plantsman.

Unlike other aspects of horticulture, water gardening presents itself as a self-contained entity, a microcosm of our world where plants and creatures depend upon one another for their continued existence. It is this which both fascinates and frustrates, for when it works and the pool is in balance it is a magical place, but where the balance is not achieved the water garden can become a nightmare. It is the blending of the essential and the decorative into a cohesive whole, and learning to manage both effectively, that is the key to success with water gardening.

With the information that is available through these pages, the mystery of the underwater world is revealed and its successful management explained. Getting things right to begin with saves a lot of heartache later. Once the foundations are laid and the principles understood, the rest is child's play. All you have to do then is to enjoy your creation. Sit beside the pool surrounded by the waxy beauty of water-lily blossoms, dabbling your fingers in the warm water as the goldfish rise for flies. A blissful experience that in reality is not difficult to achieve. P.S.

ACKNOWLEDGEMENTS

The publishers would like to thank the following for supplying photographs for this book: Garden Picture Library: pp. 4, 5, 9, 16, 17, 20, 21, 25, 28, 36, 40, 57, 73, 77, 81, 84, 85 (bottom); Jerry Harpur: pp. 8, 53; Clive Nichols: pp. 41, 48, 61, 68, 85 (top), 88; Hugh Palmer: pp. 32, 33, 44, 65; Photos Horticultural Picture Library: p. 45; Harry Smith: p. 37; Wildlife Matters: pp. 29 (top), 60, 80

The line illustrations were drawn by Jonathan Adams and Nils Solberg.

· 1 ·
Creating a Water Garden

Once a pool has been constructed it is virtually immovable, so great care has to be taken from the outset to ensure that it is situated in a position where it is not only aesthetically pleasing, but where it can function properly.

Selecting a site

A pool is a complete miniature underwater world where plants and livestock depend upon one another for their continued existence, so conditions have to be provided that enable each to develop to their full potential. Part of this can be achieved by the shape and internal structure of the pool, but its position within the garden is equally important.

In order to prosper, all popular aquatic plants demand full sunlight. There are one or two that have some tolerance of shade, but these are the least pleasing species which are normally only considered where an existing pool in a difficult position has to be coped with. Certainly the popular water-lilies, aquatic iris and marsh marigolds are intolerant of any but the most minimal of shade.

It is important to check the position regarding light during the summer when the foliage is on nearby trees. If you assess a site for light during the winter, take into account the potential for shading when any trees are in full leaf.

The shade cast by buildings is somewhat different. If the area is shaded during the summer, then it is of no use for a water garden, but care should be taken when looking at a site in the winter, for the shaded area may just be the result of the sun being low in the sky. Full sunlight during the winter months is of little importance for the pool, it is only when the plants are in active growth that it is vital. During the summer season, when the sun is high in the sky, a shaded winter site may be bathed in sunshine.

Exposed sites are not desirable, even though they are likely to be in full sun. A blustery spot creates enormous difficulties for container-grown marginal aquatics which continually blow over and land in the water. When reinstated they always look drab and often have vestiges of algae and other aquatic debris clinging to them.

Evaporation is also greater from a water surface that is exposed to wind. This may not be as significant during the summer as evaporation, but it is certainly a factor to consider. The more that water loss can be prevented, the less likely it is that algal problems will occur. The constant topping up of a pond with fresh water introduces new mineral salts upon which green water-discolouring algae feed.

A site where evaporation is significant is often likely to be cold as well. While a low temperature is not going to cause serious problems, most pool owners prefer to have as short a period of ice cover on the pool as possible. Certainly there are artificial means of rendering such conditions safe

◄ Natural pools have a lot to offer the thoughtful planter, but they are trickier to maintain.

► A formal garden requires a water garden of formal aspect, the outline reflecting that of other garden features.

for the fish, but the shorter the period that ice is present, the better.

Exposed places are not necessarily the coldest in the garden. Frost pockets often occur in sheltered low-lying parts from where cold air cannot escape. These areas should also be avoided.

Get to know where the water table lies in your garden during the wettest winter months. The soil is about as saturated as it is likely to become during late winter and you can easily establish where it is by digging a hole. From a visual point of view a pool is often best placed in the lower part of the landscape; however, this is where the water table will be found at its highest.

If it is just beneath the surface of the soil some drainage arrangements will have to be made to release its potential for pressure on the pool. If a pool liner is installed in a part of a garden where there is no drainage and a high water table, then the external water pressure will be such that it balloons the liner out into the pool.

There is no guarantee that a drain in the vicinity will alleviate this pressure completely, but it can make a localized difference. This is equally important for pre-formed pools, for ground water pressure is quite capable of lifting these out of their excavation if precautions are not taken. In certain circumstances, especially when it is known that a low-lying part of the garden becomes regularly sodden or flooded during the winter it will be better to select an alternative site.

Even if normal ground water can be relieved from a structure it is sometimes ill-advised to place a pool in a low-lying position because of the potential for flooding during the winter or following summer storms.

DESIGNING A WATER GARDEN

For a water feature to rest easily in a garden it must conform to the overall design. A formal pool with straight lines or definite curves and arcs is ill at ease unless in a formal garden setting (Fig. 1), while an informal pool which is a happy tangle of plants is better suited to a cottage garden style of gardening.

Water used for water's sake is the prerogative of the formal feature, whether it be still and reflective or water sculpture, for with the clever use of fountain jets it is possible to produce what amounts to a moving, watery artistic feature.

Still water

The reflecting pool has long been a major tool of garden designers, being used to create an air of tranquillity as well as a means of giving an illusion of space. Even quite a small body of water can make a garden seem much larger, reflecting nearby trees and the ever-changing pattern of the sky. A mirror that is only disturbed by the occasional antics of the fish. Such a mirror can be used deliberately to reflect a statue or strategically placed group of plants to great effect. Alternatively it can be left completely uncluttered, just surrounded by well mown grass.

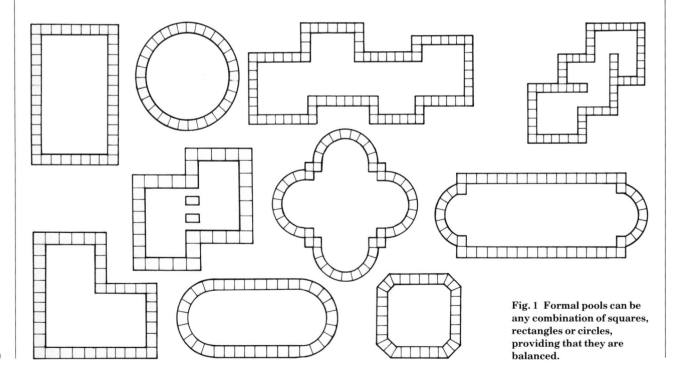

Fig. 1 Formal pools can be any combination of squares, rectangles or circles, providing that they are balanced.

The trickery which can be perpetrated on the eye by a mirror of water is further enhanced when it disappears behind a planting. In the grand landscapes of the past this has been a common practice, but in a small garden it can be effective too, such as a finger of water which disappears behind a small group of shrubs.

Other illusions which can be created with still water include the lengthening of a foreshortened garden by the use of a slender canal. The great designer Edwin Lutyens used this technique to perfection with his long, narrow water features which were uncluttered by plants, except in occasional groups along the edges. He not only used narrow water features of regular formality, but would often narrow the canal at the far end to give an illusion of distance. This illusion was enhanced by the placing of groups of shrubs at irregular intervals along either side as if the feature were leading out into the countryside.

Of course, most of the gardens of Lutyens were on a grand scale, but the principles that he adopted can be very effective, even on a small suburban plot. It is here that width rather than length is likely to present the gardener with problems, for many gardens are on the narrow side. Using a similar technique a garden can be made to appear wider by taking a narrow water feature across its width (Fig. 2). In this case it is important to leave it largely free of upstanding aquatics as these diminish the effect. Instead choose water-lilies and other deep-water aquatics, but use them sparingly as the reflective water surface is the main contributor to the illusion of space.

Water can also be used to link various parts of the garden. It may culminate in a pool, but a stream or channel can be very effective alone. The Chinese were great exponents of the use of water to create and unravel mysteries, the trickling and

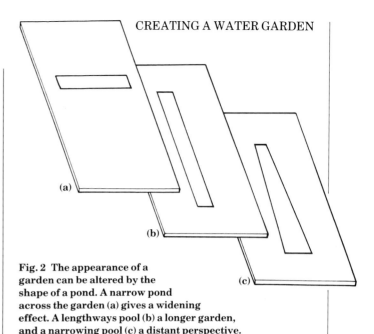

Fig. 2 The appearance of a garden can be altered by the shape of a pond. A narrow pond across the garden (a) gives a widening effect. A lengthways pool (b) a longer garden, and a narrowing pool (c) a distant perspective.

tumbling of water leading the visitor from one part of the garden to another, often disappearing temporarily and then suddenly re-appearing.

Again the scale of what the Chinese created is beyond anything that the home gardener can hope for, but the feel of mystery and tranquillity achieved by a sliver of silvery water moving from one part of the garden to another is quite simple to create. The passage of water from rock garden to pool or via a small stream overhung with plants is most effective.

Japanese water gardening depends upon symbolism. In some cases it is clearly comprehensible: the idea of digging a pool to the shape of an animal may not be our idea of a suitable feature for a suburban garden but the representation is obvious. Other Japanese water garden features, although full of symbolism, are only fully understood by those who make a study of the subject. For most western gardeners the Japanese style is what is adopted and this only fits in where the remainder of the garden has an oriental flavour.

11

The shallow, perfectly sculpted pool with cobble floor and strategically placed stone lantern, accompanied by neatly clipped shrubs and occasional marginal planting can become a reality in a small garden, but it essentially captures the atmosphere of Japan rather than recreating accurate symbolism.

Increasingly this kind of water feature is seen in conjunction with the keeping of Japanese Koi carp, a craze which has swept the western world in recent times.

Water is an essential feature of a Japanese garden, helping to create an atmosphere of quiet contemplation.

● *Wildlife pool* A complete visual contrast is provided by the wildlife pool, although the philosophy is perhaps not unlike that of the Japanese feature: a communion and celebration of and with nature. The wildlife pool tends to be more practical, its purpose being to provide a safe haven for wildlife which in turn can yield a point of interest for the gardener.

Visually, the wildlife water feature has little to commend it, unless your garden is very informal and perhaps with a view of open country. It is usually an unsightly tangle that is best hidden from view if the remainder of your garden is well manicured.

While a wildlife pool will unquestionably yield the greatest diversity of wildlife, a straightforward garden pool that is carefully balanced with attractive aquatic plants of garden merit will play host to a wide range of aquatic fauna. For most gardeners this is the happiest compromise.

Moving water

The ways in which water can be used in the garden are numerous. While the flat mirror-like surface of a still pool has much to commend it, there are also many ingenious ways in which water can be utilized as a moving feature, creating both visual effects and sound. However, before embarking upon any such feature it is wise to reflect upon the restrictions that this places on the cultivation of aquatics. Water-lilies and most other deep water aquatics dislike moving water and so must be excluded.

● *Modern pumps* have revolutionized the moving of water, especially the small submersible kinds which are placed in the water and merely plugged into the electricity supply. While surface pumps are sometimes necessary for moving large volumes of water, for most home gardeners the days of needing a specially constructed pump chamber have passed.

The efficiency and compactness of modern pumps has also added to the versatility which the gardener now has to pursue his ideas. While innovation is always welcomed, it is amongst traditional moving water features that most gardeners are at home. With a small pool either the simple fountain or waterfall.

Both are easily introduced, but there should be an awareness that with the small water feature their presence will create considerable constraints upon the plant material that it is possible to grow.

Modern pumps have a simple range of fittings that can produce almost any configuration of fountain spray that is desired, from delicate water bells to foaming geysers. Thus the pump with a specially manufactured nozzle is immediately a fountain. Remove the nozzle and replace with a hosepipe and the pump immediately turns into a water source for a waterfall or gargoyle.

Of course fountains can be much more elaborate than water jets erupting from the pool. A wide range of ornaments are available into which the output of the pump can be connected. Some of these ornaments are prepared with fountain jets to give the most appropriate effect, but in many cases you can choose the best spray pattern for your own situation.

An ornament can consist of a cherub or dolphin spouting water from a convenient place, but it can equally be a more elaborate structure from which water issues and tumbles from one basin to another. To recreate the feel of the classical garden in suburbia only demands the purchase of a replica ornament made of reconstituted stone, it being placed in position and connected to a submersible pump. The elaborate engineering requirements of years gone by no longer apply.

Where space is at a premium fountains need not shoot spray into the air, but merely bubble. Bubbling features which are completely safe for children are a method of bringing the benefits of moving water into the most restricted space. Some bubble fountains are created beneath old millstones surrounded by gravel, the pump being hidden in a chamber beneath. An urn can serve a similar purpose.

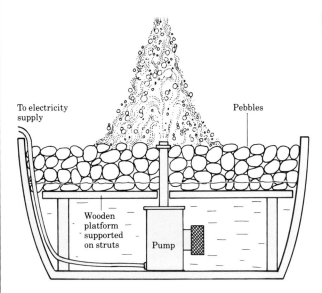

To electricity supply

Pebbles

Wooden platform supported on struts

Pump

Fig. 3 A half-barrel with a submersible pump installed and a generous layer of pebbles is a safe way of having moving water.

Provided it can accommodate a pump, which in turn is completely submerged by water, an arrangement can be made by which a strong wire mesh cover is fitted across the top of the urn, but just beneath the upper edge. It is then covered with carefully selected stones or cobbles and the fountain spray passes up through this (Fig. 3).

The limitations of space can also be overcome by the use of masks, gargoyles and wall fountains. From the elaborate mask arrangement with semi-circular basal pool to the small hanging wall fountain with self-contained pump, there are opportunities for everyone to enjoy a small spout or fountain. Not only this, but with slight adaptations our traditional ways of moving water, especially in small spaces, can be adjusted to accept the traditions of other cultures, for example by utilizing bamboo pipes we can bring a Japanese flavour to our garden.

Preparing the site

The size of the hole to be excavated to accommodate a pool will depend upon the method of construction to be used. With a liner pool the excavation is of exactly the same size and contours as the finished feature, whereas with a concrete structure the hole is 15 cm (6 in) larger all round to allow for the thickness of the concrete. On the other hand a pre-formed pool will not demand an excavation of the same shape and size, but a large hole that will comfortably embrace the extremes of length, breadth and depth of the pool.

While you may have the design of a pool in mind, or may have sketched ideas out on paper, unless the pool is of a predetermined size it will prove necessary to create and view the shape on the ground. Unless you happen to have a very good artistic eye it is unlikely that you will be able to determine the final dimensions without making some adjustments. Formality and informality may well have been decided, but it is essential to view the potential pool in outline before taking to the spade.

Creating a shape

To create a suitable outline for a pool that is to be constructed with a liner or concrete, take a length of rope or malleable hose-pipe and lay it on the ground in the desired shape. View the pool from both the garden and the house to confirm that it is pleasing from all angles. It is useful to take a look from upstairs too before making a final commitment. What looks attractive at ground level may not be so acceptable when viewed from above.

If the pool is to be placed in the lawn and there is the possibility of grass growing up to the water's edge at some point, ensure that the curves and arcs of the pool outline are such that the turf can be mown successfully. Run the lawnmower around the outline. This is not only important for those pools where grass meets water, but also other kinds which may be heavily planted around the edge. The sweep of the domestic lawnmower is conveniently the same as the arc or curve that accommodates the pool liner without unsightly wrinkles and approximates to the most convenient outline for concrete pool construction without the necessity for shuttering.

Marking out

Once the shape has been finalized, mark it out with short wooden stakes. Unless the site is accurately angled, stakes of 30 cm (12 in) which will permit a maximum of 23 cm (9 in) to remain above ground, are adequate. When putting these in, ensure that they are level with one another across the pool's excavation. Use a stout plank of wood stood on edge with a spirit level placed upon it. Place the plank on two adjacent pegs, knocking the higher peg down with a hammer until it is level with the other. This is indicated by the bubble in the spirit level resting exactly between the two central lines.

The levelling operation must commence with the peg which is situated in the lowest part of the excavation. It need not be knocked into the ground down to ground level as this may create difficulties with transferring levels.

If the pool is of a pre-determined shape, it is relatively easy to mark it out on the ground.

● *An oblong or square pool* When the pool is to be oblong or square, hammer in two stakes to form the length of one side. In the case of an oblong pool choose the longer side. Be sure that this is parallel with any wall or path that it is intended to associate with by measuring from the path or wall to each stake. The measurements should be identical. Attach a string to each peg and then pull it tight. This is the base line from which the remainder of the pool is marked out (Fig. 4).

To ensure that the next side is marked out as an exact right angle measure 90 cm (3 ft) along the string of the base line. Hammer in a peg and knock a small nail into the top. Take the string for the next side and measure 1.2 m (4 ft) along its length. Attach a string to the nail in the top of the other peg along the base line and measure 1.5 m (5 ft). Bring the two marked lengths together (a). Where they meet knock a peg into the ground. The string for the second side should be extended to the length of the side, passing directly over the peg at the meeting point. The angle where the two sides meet will be a right angle. Repeat this for the other corners. To check that the four corner pegs represent right angles, check the diagonals between. They should be the same length.

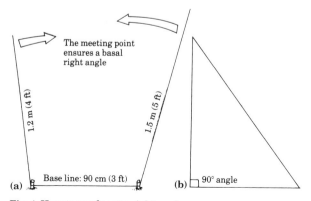

The meeting point ensures a basal right angle

1.2 m (4 ft)

1.5 m (5 ft)

Base line: 90 cm (3 ft)

(a)

(b) 90° angle

Fig. 4 How to mark out a right angle.

15

◄ This formal pool has been strikingly enhanced by the restrained introduction and careful placing of aquatic plants.

▶ A tastefully planted
informal pool which rests
easily in the landscape. Note
the easy access in the
foreground.

● *A circular pool* is the simplest to mark out (Fig. 5a). Determine where you would like the centre of the pool to be and knock in a stake. Attach a string to the stake the length of the intended radius of the pool. To the end secure a pointed bamboo cane or stake. Pull the string taut and inscribe a circle in the ground by walking with the string around the centre stake.

● *An oval pool* (Fig. 5b) can be marked out by determining the centre and then first knocking in a stake. Mark each end of the oval with stakes in a similar way. Put two further stakes in line with the centre and end stakes at a point two-thirds of the distance from these centre and end stakes. Do this at each end. Cut string and make a loop that will just fit round either of these stakes to the stake farthest from it. Using the centre three stakes, take up the slack and keep the string tight while walking around the stakes, marking the ground with a sharp stick held against the string. This, if continued around, will automatically produce an oval shape.

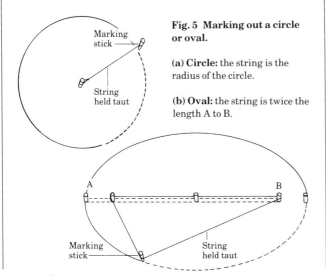

Marking stick →

String held taut

A

B

Marking stick

String held taut

Fig. 5 Marking out a circle or oval.

(a) Circle: the string is the radius of the circle.

(b) Oval: the string is twice the length A to B.

A water feature on a sloping site

When excavating a pool on a sloping site it is important to ensure that the installation is level, even if advantage is to be taken of the landfall. If the site is to be completely levelled, then there is no problem, for once the ground is levelled the pool can be marked out and excavated in the usual way.

Where the slope is being used within the design, level off an area sufficiently large to accommodate the pool and a small working area. 30 cm (12 in) all round is usually sufficient. Knock in level pegs and using a spirit level and board, create a profile of the landfall. With a spade remove all the soil from the enlarged outline of the pool until the distance from the top of each level peg to the excavated soil surface is the same. The base is then level and the pool can be marked out in the normal way.

Sometimes soil will be introduced to level a sloping site partially, or a retaining wall be thought desirable at the lower end of the slope. When this is the case the same system of pegs is used.

Raised ponds

Not all ponds need to be in the ground. Indeed, for the less active a raised pond has many advantages, particularly of accessibility. In some garden designs it is very necessary, particularly where it is to be associated with a sitting-out area.

Raised pools involve the same considerations as those in the ground, although because of their exposure to the extremes of the elements it is wise to make them steep-sided and as deep as possible, although marginal shelves can be accommodated. The means of support for the liner can be varied from brickwork and stone walls to timber. The latter is the simplest method for the home gardener (Fig. 6).

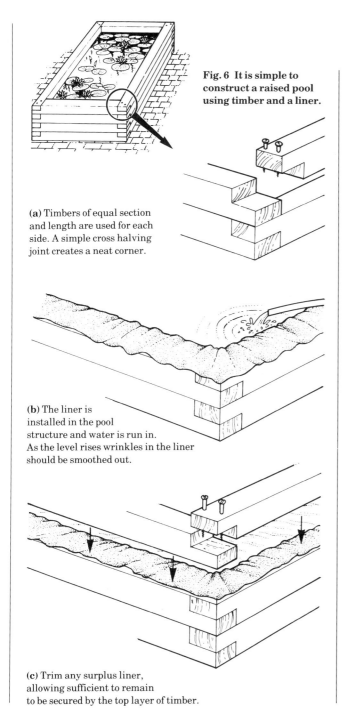

Fig. 6 It is simple to construct a raised pool using timber and a liner.

(a) Timbers of equal section and length are used for each side. A simple cross halving joint creates a neat corner.

(b) The liner is installed in the pool structure and water is run in. As the level rises wrinkles in the liner should be smoothed out.

(c) Trim any surplus liner, allowing sufficient to remain to be secured by the top layer of timber.

A timber surround can be of sawn or rough wood and cut into any configuration desired. While a raised square or oblong pool may be traditional, there are great opportunities for producing hexagons or octagons and other mathematical shapes.

Cut the timbers to length for the various sides. Notch them together so that they fit neatly, removing part of the end of one piece of timber to accommodate the remaining part of its neighbour. This amounts to a halving joint. The timbers can be fastened together with dowels, screwed or attached to corner posts.

Using a set square, ensure that the corners of the structure are square or of equal angles. Once the structure is secured, square and level, the liner can be installed.

Raised pools can be constructed from brick with a concrete base. It is a professional job to build the low walls which provide the pool structure. These should be constructed so that fish and plants can survive the winter unharmed. A minimum depth of 60 cm (2 ft) is desirable. Where the edge of the pool is to be lower, then the pool can be partially sunk into the ground. The depth is of no consequence on the outside, but vital inside.

Once a structure has been completed, the inside of the walls are rendered with a waterproof concrete mixture. This again is best left to the professional to ensure a watertight finish. It takes considerable skill to plaster vertical walls.

As with a concrete pool, it is important that a rendered pool does not dry out too quickly. Spray recently plastered walls with water from a watering can with a fine rose attached, or protect from drying with damp sacking or polythene.

While the pre-formed pool is not free-standing, there is no reason why it cannot be installed within a brick or stonework raised structure. All the rules of back filling and levelling apply.

◄ A raised pool provides the opportunity to observe fish and other aquatic life at close quarters.

▶ In a small courtyard water can be effectively introduced, at the same time providing a simple focal point.

· 2 ·
Constructing
a Water Garden

There is still a great urge amongst many gardeners to have a natural earth-bottom pool. This is a romantic viewpoint and understandable, but it is certainly not the most practical method of construction, nor the easiest kind of water feature to maintain. Even a pool that is completely natural and merely needs decorating with suitable plants will inevitably create problems not encountered with artificial methods of construction.

THE NATURAL POOL

With a natural earth pond the greatest difficulty is maintaining a suitable water level. Even on soil that is a heavy and almost impervious clay, this can be a problem unless there is a natural water source like a stream or spring nearby that can be depended upon to replace water that is lost by seepage.

The traditional method of waterproofing an earth pond is by puddling it with clay. This is not a very satisfactory method of construction, for throughout its life a clay-puddled pool needs to be kept filled to the top or any exposed area of puddle regularly watered to keep it supple.

While in some circumstances a puddled clay pond can function effectively owing to an easily regulated input of water, it should be remembered that its life is likely to be limited on account of the vigorous nature of aquatic plant life. Boisterous species such as *Sparganium* and *Typha* have strong, vigorous root systems which are quite capable of puncturing the best puddled ponds. They and other vigorous marginal subjects also grow into the puddle, thereby destroying its effectiveness when it is time to lift and divide the plants. The entire puddling process then needs to be repeated.

Choosing clay

The correct amount and quality of clay used in a puddled pond are vital to its success. A pond should have a minimum depth of 15 cm (6 in) of clay, so the excavation must be 15 cm (6 in) larger than the finished pool. Add to this quantity a further one third for bulking. This is about the quantity of air that will be present in an uncompressed load of clay.

In addition to natural local clays there are two other kinds of bentonite clays which are specifically marketed for industrial purposes and can be used. Both are available as fine powders which swell on contact with water to form an impermeable gel. The first, sodium clay, swells to about 15 times it own volume while the second, calcium clay, increases to about 8 times its dry volume.

THE POOL LINER (Fig. 7)

All pool liners are installed in a similar manner, those manufactured from polythene being spread out on the lawn in the sun for an hour or two before work begins. They then become supple and mould more readily to the excavation.

Preparing the excavation

Scour the hole thoroughly for sharp stones, twigs or any other objects that may puncture the liner once it is subjected to the weight and pressure of the water. Even quite small rough stones can be forced through a liner and will cause a leak.

Cover the floor of the excavation and the marginal shelves with a generous layer of sand. Use soft builders' sand, for when this is dampened it can also be used effectively to 'plaster' the walls of the excavation, even if they are almost vertical.

An alternative is to use old pieces of carpet as a protective lining, but these often show through the liner as lumps and creases. Thick wads of old newspaper that have been dampened can also be utilized for the same purpose. However, this is of short duration, as the newspaper usually deteriorates within three or four years.

Many garden centres sell a special fleece for pre-lining the excavation. This is durable, relatively easy to install and does not show, but it is a more expensive method. Spread the fleece out as evenly and wrinkle-free as possible across the whole excavation.

Installing the liner

Polythene liners have little elasticity and so must be installed without water being added. Allow plenty of room for movement so that when water is eventually added the wrinkles can be more easily smoothed out and the liner moulded to the exact contours of the hole. Spread the liner over

Fig. 7 Constructing a pool using a PVC or rubber liner.

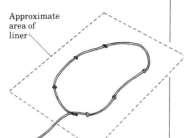

Approximate area of liner

(a) Mark out the shape of the pool with a rope and peg in position.

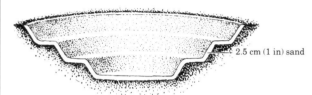

2.5 cm (1 in) sand

(b) Excavate the pool to slightly larger than the desired shape and add a layer of sand.

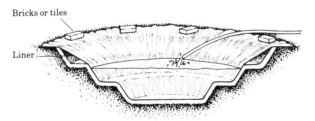

Bricks or tiles

Liner

(c) Install the liner, running water into the pool to help the liner mould to the contours.

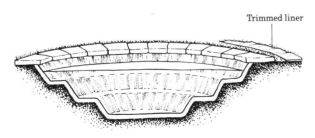

Trimmed liner

(d) Trim off the excess liner mould and finish with paving stones.

23

the excavation making sure that it is arranged so that there is sufficient material to spread up the marginal areas. It is often deceptive as to how off-centre a liner needs to be placed over an irregular pool to ensure that it fits snugly with sufficient overlap all round.

The same arrangement applies to rubber or PVC liners, although they are easier to install, the principle being to stretch the liner across the hole, weighing the edges down with rocks or paving slabs. Add water and as the liner tightens slowly release the anchoring weights around the pool until it becomes full and the liner moulds to its exact shape.

While this is slowly taking place, smooth out the wrinkles in the liner, working systematically around the pool. Even with a simple shape some folds will be necessary. Make these few but bold rather than small and numerous. Large folds are scarcely discernible if neatly made and within a short time blend into the background.

The edge can be secured by a row of paving slabs which trap the liner beneath paving and soil. Once the edge of the liner has been firmly secured any surplus material should be cut away.

THE PRE-FORMED POOL (Fig. 8)

One of the most frequent assumptions made by those new to water gardening, and regrettably amongst many of those who sell pre-formed pools as well, is that installation is merely a question of dropping the pool into a prepared hole the exact shape of the pool shell.

Nothing could be further from the truth. It is virtually impossible to dig an accurate shape without very detailed measurements. In any event, the installation of a pre-formed pool requires a much larger hole than the finished pool size if it is to be introduced painlessly.

Preparing the hole

Dig a sufficiently large hole to embrace the maximum dimensions of the pre-formed pool. Also allow sufficient extra space for comfortable backfilling once the pool is in position in the excavation. This means that you usually have to dig quite a large rectangular hole.

Spread a layer of sand over the floor of the excavation so that the pool can rest evenly on this. A depth of 2.5 cm (1 in) is sufficient. Place the pool in the hole and level it from end to end and side to side with a plank on edge and a spirit level. Some parts of the pool will need supporting as they are much shallower. Place bricks beneath these to adjust the height and provide support. These can remain in the hole during backfilling.

It is vital that the pool is level from end to end and side to side. Leave it about 2.5 cm (1 in) below the level of the finished surrounding ground level. This ensures that when backfilling takes place that the lifting of the pool, which is inevitable, leaves the structure at ground level and not above.

Backfilling

You can backfill with excavated soil, but in most cases this is too coarse and lumpy to do a good job. It is important that the backfilling flows around the contours of the pre-formed shape. Sand can be used, but fine gravel, such as that referred to as pea gravel, is far superior.

It is important to provide complete support for the prefabricated shape. Not only does the weight of water within have the potential to cause fracturing with a fibreglass pool if it is not properly supported, but more especially does the

▶ **Marginal plants such as irises are used successfully in this pool to disguise an ugly liner.**

Fig. 8 Installing a pre-formed pool.

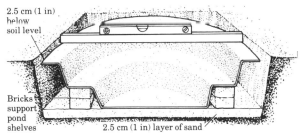

2.5 cm (1 in)
below
soil level

Bricks
support
pond
shelves

2.5 cm (1 in) layer of sand

(a) Excavate a rectangular pool which is greater than both the length and width, installing the pool carefully supported on bricks.

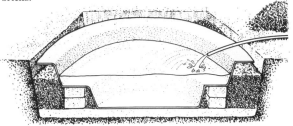

(b) Backfill with gravel, in the case of a flexible plastic pool running water into it at the same time being sure to keep both gravel and water levels equal.

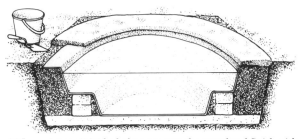

(c) Lay a 2.5 cm (1 in) bed of mortar over the gravel and finish with paving.

(d) Carefully position the paving stones so that they slightly overhang the pool edge.

heavy boot of the gardener if he decides at some future date to clean out the pool and finds it necessary to stand in it.

During backfilling, regularly check the level of the pool. Backfill in a systematic way, working around the pool. This causes the minimum of deviation in the levels. Gently flow the gravel or backfill between the pool structure and excavation.

Flexible pools

Some pre-formed pools are made of a thin plastic material. These are very durable, but also flexible. If placed in the hole and backfilled in the manner just described they twist and buckle. The only method of keeping them in shape is to add water as backfilling takes place.

Regulate the flow of water so that the internal water level and the external backfilling are constantly kept equal. If one overtakes the other the pool will distort.

Before running in water check that the edge of the pool is level with the surrounding ground. By adding the weight of water from the beginning this kind of pool does not rise as backfilling takes place.

An alternative method of installing a pre-formed pool is to place the shape in position on the site, propping it up with bricks or lengths of wood. Transfer the position of the outer edge of the pool to the ground by placing a spirit level next to it, pushing wooden pegs into the soil at intervals of about 30 cm (12 in) as you work systematically around it.

Remove the pre-formed shape and dig around the outside of the pegs, about 10 cm (4 in) away, removing them as you progress. When the excavation is of the required dimensions add a layer of sand and firm the base and shelves by treading. Lower the pre-formed shape into the excavation and press it firmly into a sand base.

THE CONCRETE POOL

Until fairly recent times it used to be thought necessary to construct a permanent pool in concrete. Indeed, even today there are those who advocate it above all other methods for its apparent permanence. This is a myth, for while concrete can indeed be permanent and solid, it can equally fall to pieces within twelve months if not properly constructed. For most gardeners concrete is the prerogative of the professional who is fully aware of its properties and problems. Only a good do-it-yourself amateur is likely to make a satisfactory job.

In addition to the heavy work that is involved and the fact that an excavation at least 15 cm (6 in) deeper than the finished pool is necessary to accommodate the layer of concrete, it is the most difficult material to get watertight and the most toxic to fish and plant life. Both aspects demand treatment.

Without recourse to complex timber shuttering arrangements, the shapes and angles that can be created are very limited with concrete compared with a pool liner. There is also greater vulnerability to leaking, especially on heavy clay soil which shrinks during hot summer weather. Unless the concrete is very well laid, then the chances of fractures appearing are rather high unless the construction is laid on a generous raft of sand. Even then there is no guarantee against movement affecting the structure.

While the advantages of concrete are few for the home gardener, it does come into its own where moving water is to be introduced and a heavy fountain ornament is to be installed. While it is possible to position a paving slab both beneath the liner and on top of it to provide some stability, it is not as successful as a solid concrete base. This is not necessary for the standard small fountain ornaments that are available from the garden centre.

An attractive finish can be provided by concrete in pools and other water features where water is the priority rather than plants or fish (in turbulent moving-water features or the reflective pond for example). Concrete does not have to be a dull soulless grey, with the addition of colourants it can be made most appealing.

Mix the ingredients that are to provide the various colours into the concrete at the dry-mix stage. Only use the coloured mix for the final 5 cm (2 in) layer. These pigments can be incorporated in with the cement in any proportion up to 10 per cent by weight to ensure a good even colouring. Red oxide provides a red colouring, chromium oxide a deep green, cobalt blue a blue and manganese black a black, while the use of snowcrete cement and fine Derbyshire spar produces a first-class white finish.

Concrete installation

The excavation for a concrete pool must be 15 cm (6 in) larger than the finished pool. For the concrete pool to be successful it must have at least a 15 cm (6 in) layer of concrete.

The shape of the pool should be marked out on the ground using a rope, hosepipe or strings in the same manner as when creating an excavation for

◄ **Wooden decking extending from the edge of the pool over the water provides a delightful sitting-out area.**

► **The patterned edging of cobbles, bricks and slabs provides colour and contrast to the still water of a reflecting pool.**

▼ (*Left*) **Irregular cobbles can be used as a feature to hide the edge of the pool.**

▼ (*Right*) **It is essential to have access to the pool. Crazy paving is the easiest on the eye with an informal pool.**

29

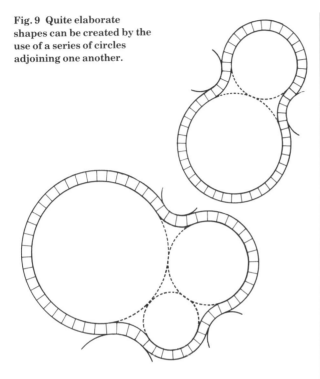

Fig. 9 Quite elaborate shapes can be created by the use of a series of circles adjoining one another.

a pool liner. Unless you have drawn all your garden out on graph paper it is unnecessary to provide a design on paper. Even if this is wholly accurate it is unlikely to look how you expect it will unless you have a very good imagination. Even then minor adjustments will be necessary.

First of all dig the excavation to the size and shape of the desired pool. This presents an accurate picture of what the feature will eventually look like and allows for alterations to be made. Assessing how much soil to remove from the walls is simple as a line can be strung out 15 cm (6 in) back from the face of the initial excavation. The floor is more difficult, but accuracy is most simply achieved by taking stakes that are longer than 15 cm (6 in) and knocking them into the ground so that the tops are protruding about 2.5 cm (1 in) above the surface. Knock these into the ground at random, but ensure that they are all level with one another by transferring levels with a board and spirit level. It is then possible during excavation to measure accurately downwards from each stake to obtain a reference point for the desired depth. Once the excavation is complete the stakes are discarded. The same system can be used for any shallow areas or shelves.

For a regular pool that is being constructed without shuttering (Fig. 10), the slopes of the hole should be at an angle of no more than 45°. Steeper sides preclude the concrete from remaining in place. This is especially true when a polythene membrane is introduced between the soil and the wet concrete. A steep slope will cause it to slide down the polythene.

Once the excavation has been completed the surface of the soil must be tamped down firmly. If the floor of the pool is soft and muddy, introduce hardcore to a depth of about 15 cm (6 in) and ram it down firmly.

Polythene membrane
Builders' polythene is a very heavy gauge material which is introduced to the excavation like a pool liner. It serves as an additional line of defence in preventing leaking, but is more important at construction time in preventing the rapid loss of moisture into the surrounding soil. If the concrete loses water too quickly it is likely to crack. What is required is a slow drying out.

Scour the hole for any obvious sharp stones or other objects that may puncture the polythene when the weight of concrete is added. Place the polythene in the hole and mould it to the shape of the excavation. If it wrinkles a little in the corners it does not matter as it will be completely hidden by the concrete.

Introducing the concrete

Introduce the first layer of concrete to a depth of 10 cm (4 in) and trowel it evenly over the whole pool. A layer of 5 cm (2 in) mesh-wire netting, such as used for poultry, can then be introduced as a reinforcing layer. Spread the netting over the concrete and push it slightly into the wet mixture ensuring that where two pieces of netting join there is an overlap of 10 cm (4 in). The final layer of 5 cm (2 in) of concrete is then laid over the top. If there is to be a coloured finish, it is incorporated into this layer.

Trowel the surface smooth to create the desired finish. Once complete protect the surface from rapid drying out by placing damp sacks or hessian over the surface. When this is not available, then a regular watering regime will have to be invoked. This is less desirable than being able to cover the surface of the concrete with sacking or similar material.

Where watering is the only option, this consists of fitting up the watering can with a very fine rose and periodically sprinkling the surface of the concrete to prevent it from drying out completely. The frequency with which this will need to be done will depend upon the weather. Dampening is all that is needed; running water will effectively dilute the mixture and also create rivulets or a coarse gritty finish to the surface of the concrete, which in turn makes it vulnerable to damage by winter weather. This prevents the concrete from drying out too quickly. When this happens hair cracks appear all over the surface and if these become more pronounced can cause the start of leakage problems. For the most part they are hair-like and affect the surface of the pool. They cause no serious concern as regards leakage, but with the coming of winter and the prospect of sharp frost they often lead to the flaking and crumbling of the surface. This in itself will not

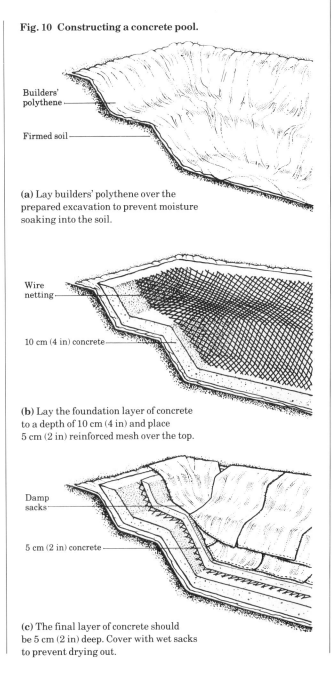

Fig. 10 Constructing a concrete pool.

Builders' polythene

Firmed soil

(a) Lay builders' polythene over the prepared excavation to prevent moisture soaking into the soil.

Wire netting

10 cm (4 in) concrete

(b) Lay the foundation layer of concrete to a depth of 10 cm (4 in) and place 5 cm (2 in) reinforced mesh over the top.

Damp sacks

5 cm (2 in) concrete

(c) The final layer of concrete should be 5 cm (2 in) deep. Cover with wet sacks to prevent drying out.

◄ Although very functional, the harshness of concrete is not easy to disguise, even when heavily planted.

► This octagonal pool is greatly enhanced by the strategic placement of water-lilies, but the open areas of water are equally important.

cause water to leak away, but as each winter passes the surface crumbles a little more and the whole pool begins to deteriorate.

Covering the surface of the concrete to prevent drying out too quickly will ensure a hard, almost glossy surface that is impervious to the elements.

Shuttering (Fig. 11)

More sophisticated pools, that is pools that are of formal aspect with upright or steeply angled sides require shuttering. Shuttering is usually made from timber and effectively forms a mould into which concrete is poured and shaped. It is not a method of construction for the uninitiated, for it demands not only considerable knowledge, but a relatively high degree of practical skill.

Shuttering timbers need to be substantial, even for a small pool with relatively little concrete. The pressure of concrete tamped down behind a shutter board is considerable and so strong external bracing is required.

Prepare the shuttering well ahead of concreting so that when the floor has been completed the shutter boards and supporting timbers can be quickly installed. In some cases it is possible to raise the wall shutter slightly so that the concrete of the wall can flow beneath and unite with the floor. It is necessary to contrive this when any extensive shuttering is proposed. Shuttering is put together as a prefabricated structure. Which means each wall mould should be prepared and nailed in place.

33

Fig. 11 Shuttering is vital for pools with upright or steeply angled sides where the wet concrete would have no support.

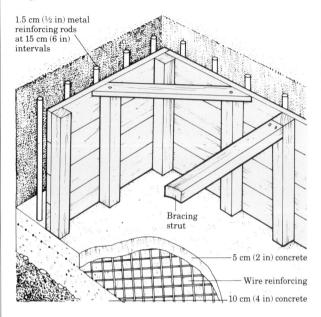

1.5 cm (½ in) metal reinforcing rods at 15 cm (6 in) intervals

Bracing strut

5 cm (2 in) concrete

Wire reinforcing

10 cm (4 in) concrete

Lay the floor in the conventional way putting down a 10 cm (4 in) layer of concrete. Place reinforcing wire over this. When shuttering is already in place in the pool it is often possible to pull the wire down the cavity of the wall on one side, across the floor and up the wall on the other side. If this is not practical push 1.5 cm (½ in) metal reinforcing rods into the floor of the pool through the centre of the proposed wall behind the shuttering. Space at 15 cm (6 in) intervals. The floor can still be reinforced with wire netting.

Once the reinforcing is in place, soak the shutter boards with water to help prevent the concrete from sticking to them. An alternative method is to paint the boards with limewash. This is a mixture of lime and water which is sufficiently thick to stick to the boards like whitewash. The concrete is then poured behind.

Laying the concrete

As the concrete is poured in, tamp it firmly with a piece of wood in order to ensure that there are no air pockets in the concrete. These could be a source of potential weakness in the walls of the pool and if situated next to the shuttering board cause irregularities in the surface of the concrete.

Leave the shuttering in place for two or three days before removing it. During the period between the concrete being poured in and the shuttering being removed, watch the concrete carefully. As with a pool that does not require shuttering support, continually dampen the concrete to prevent it from drying out too quickly and hair cracks appearing. Spray water gently over both concrete and shuttering.

Removing the shuttering

It is quite a tense moment when the shuttering is removed. Only then will you discover whether or not the concreting has been a success. Provided the concrete mixture was of the correct consistency, that it was firmed down adequately and the shutter boards were supported sufficiently with timber braces that did not move, the result will be satisfactory.

Curved shuttering

Creating a curved concrete pool is more complicated. Ordinary rough boards are too angular and difficult to use. For this kind of construction use marine plywood. This is flexible and with stout timber supports can be made to almost any curved shape that is desired. As with the more conventional shuttering this must be well braced with timbers across the pool so that it does not twist or buckle with the weight of concrete behind it. The method of concreting and striking the shuttering is exactly the same as for the more formal construction.

Sealing concrete

The greatest disadvantage of a concrete pool is the difficulty of ensuring that it is watertight and also safe for plants and fish. Concrete naturally absorbs water and also releases free lime into it when it is constructed as a pool. This is injurious to fish and also clouds the water badly. As such, finishing treatments are necessary which are not required for other construction methods.

● *Sealants* Nowadays there are sealants available which lock in the lime, sealing the concrete by a process known as internal glazing. This appears as a sugar-like fine granular material which is mixed with water and then painted on to the surface of the concrete. It does not alter the appearance of the concrete, but providing that great care is taken to ensure that coverage is complete, it has the advantage of making the pool safe for the introduction of fish and plants immediately after application.

The tub garden (Fig. 12)

Tubs and half barrels are amongst the most useful containers for a small water feature. It depends upon what they have contained, but the majority merely require scrubbing out before filling with water. Only those that have contained oil or any tar-based product need treating with caution; such tubs or barrels are best lined with a pool liner before use.

Of course, many will not have been used for anything and can be planted straight away. Be wary of new tubs that have been treated with wood preservative as this may pollute the water. If you are uncertain, then avoid such containers.

Plain wood barrels and tubs can be preserved by charring. Turn the tub on its side and run a blow torch over the interior. This creates a hard blackened surface which is resistant to decay.

Providing that they are kept damp, most tubs and barrels will remain watertight. However, this may not be possible during the winter if the water has to be emptied out and the container placed in storage. Inevitably the wood will shrink a little as it dries and leakage is then likely to occur. To overcome this possibility it is wise to line the barrel.

● *To line a tub* take a small sheet of pool liner. It is preferable to use a black rubber or PVC liner so that it will not be so readily noticed. Place the liner into the tub and make several bold folds in order to get it to fit in neatly. Do not try to distribute the folds as small wrinkles, it will look awful.

Add water in order to be sure that the liner fits snugly. Come to within about 7.5 cm (3 in) of the top of the container, allowing space for securing the liner. Use small pieces of wooden batten about 5 cm (2 in) long and 2.5 cm (1 in) wide and screw securely through this and the liner to the barrel. Do this just above the water line. Four or five of these placed equally around the top will be sufficient to fasten the lining securely.

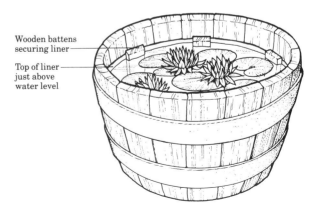

Wooden battens securing liner

Top of liner just above water level

Fig. 12 An effective water garden can be created in a wooden tub using dwarf plants.

WATER GARDENS

▶ Moving water can be successfully introduced to a small garden with a lion mask and well-planted trough.

▼ You do not need a pool to enjoy water gardening if you use suitable dwarf plants and a container.

Sinks

Old glazed sinks make excellent small water gardens. Just add the plug and they are ready for planting. Unfortunately they are very ugly in their raw state and so it is desirable to coat the sink in order to give it a stone-like appearance.

Clean the sink thoroughly and allow it to dry out. Make a mixture of 2 parts by volume moss peat, 1 part sand and 1 part cement. Add water until the mixture is stiff, but workable. It must be of such a consistency that it can be plastered on to the outer walls of the sink without sliding down.

Take a PVA (polyvinyl acetate) adhesive and spread it liberally over a portion of the sink. This serves as a bonding agent. Allow it to become tacky before plastering on the prepared mixture. Take the plastered mixture over the rim and into the sink to well below the intended water level.

It will take two weeks or so before the coating has thoroughly dried out. To begin with it looks a little raw, but the appearance of weathering can be hastened by painting the surface with a mixture of milk and manure. The exact proportions are not critical, but the mixture should be stiff enough to be applied with a brush. This encourages the rapid development of moss and algae.

The bog garden

Although it is not essential, it is usual to create a bog garden that is an integral part of the water garden. A bog can be created alone, and indeed where a pre-formed pool is being installed an adjacent bog garden has to be constructed as if it were totally separate even if it abuts the pool. There is no right or wrong shape for a bog garden, although few formal arrangements fit in well. Indeed, the bog garden and the formal water garden rarely work successfully together. The bog garden is essentially the companion of the informal water garden (Fig. 13).

This tastefully planted tub is sunk partially into the ground to provide some winter protection for the inhabitants.

It is not so critical where the bog is going to be constantly dampened by water from the pool, but even here a 30 cm (12 in) depth is desirable. Once such an excavation is lined, the area between pool and bog garden should be separated so that the soil does not muddy the water and yet the water has ready access to the bog garden soil. This can often be successfully contrived with rocks or by the use of bricks arranged in such a fashion that there are small gaps which allow the water to percolate through. Soil can be prevented from washing into the pool if a fine mesh plastic netting is trapped between the gaps in the bricks and the soil.

The soil that is introduced to the bog garden should be of a heavy nature and have plenty of well-rotted organic matter added to it. However, care should be taken to ensure that it is not so nutrient rich that it leaches minerals into the water for the benefit of green water-discolouring algae. Be guided by the recommendations made for planting aquatics and incorporate up to about a quarter by volume of organic material.

The easiest bog garden to construct utilizes a liner, either an extension of the liner being used to create the pool, or else an individual liner which is employed in a similar fashion to that used for pool construction. For an independent bog garden a polythene sheet or liner can be used. This is the cheapest material, and although it has limitations for a pool, these are not apparent with

Fig. 13 **The most effective bog garden is combined with a pool with a continuous liner.**

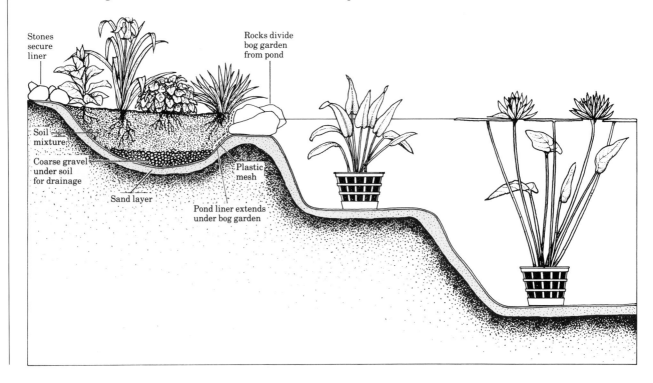

Stones secure liner

Rocks divide bog garden from pond

Soil mixture

Coarse gravel under soil for drainage

Plastic mesh

Sand layer

Pond liner extends under bog garden

· HANDY TIP ·

When creating a water feature in which the pool and the bog garden are constructed together it is important that the soil does not pollute the water. A layer of stiff fine mesh netting placed on the inside of the barrier next to the soil will prevent spillage.

a bog garden as the liner is completely covered and there are no areas exposed to sunlight which can crack and disintegrate. When a bog garden is to become an integral part of the water feature it must be considered at the same time as the pool is planned. The reason for this is that the bog will form a spreading shallow pool-like extension which will be filled with soil, but dampened by the pool water. Thus the pool and bog garden are embraced by a single membrane.

All the rules that apply to a pool are pertinent to a bog garden being made with a liner. The excavation must be scoured for sticks, stones and other objects that may puncture the lining, although the weight of soil within will bear no comparison to that of the water in a pool. Nevertheless, protection of the liner by careful preparation and the use of a sand or fleece cushion is essential.

An independent bog garden is merely a shallow excavation some 30–45 cm (12–18 in) deep which is lined and into which a heavy organic rich soil is added. It is imperative that the depth is at least 30 cm (12 in), for independent bog gardens are prone to rapid drying out and can even become drier than the surrounding ground if any shallower.

When a natural earth bottom pool has been constructed, a similar method of bog garden construction can be used with puddled clay.

Indeed a puddled clay bog garden is much more successful than a puddled pond as there is no danger of the clay being exposed to the air and cracking.

The bog requires constant moisture from the pool and so a permeable barrier between each must be erected. The most economical division is made by using stakes about 90 cm (3 ft) long and driving them into the floor of the pool at intervals of about 10 cm (4 in), at the point where the bog garden is intended to meet the pool. On the inside of this fasten a fine mesh plastic net. This permits the water entry, but prevents soil spillage into the pool. The height of the stakes when in place should be no more than 5 cm (2 in) above the level of the water in the pool.

Wildlife feature

The construction methods advocated for the decorative garden pool and bog area apply equally to wildlife features, except that the design that is preferable for wildlife is easier to achieve with a pool liner. Shallows for wading and basking as well as sudden drops to root prune invasive plants effectively are not easy to contrive with concrete and are rarely if ever found with pre-formed pools.

Many of the plants used in wildlife features are too invasive for the decorative pool, but provide just the right amount of cover for native fauna. A number are also excellent for preventing erosion or protecting against trampling, a bonus when water fowl are around.

The wildlife pool is very dependent upon a wetland surround for its success and so as much accommodation as possible should be provided. This involves extending the bog area with a liner, or with other forms of construction creating an independent bog that appears to be part of the water garden feature.

▲ A semi-natural bog garden where moisture-loving garden plants like hostas and irises have harmonized perfectly.

► A wildlife pool generously planted with reedmace, purple loosestrife and meadowsweet provides a perfect haven for native fauna.

· 3 ·
Moving Water

The ways in which moving water can be utilized in the garden are many, but the fountain is unquestionably the most spectacular. Modern submersible pumps and elaborate spray nozzles and fittings have provided the gardener with the tiniest pool the ability to create aquatic artistry of great diversity.

There is no need to live with a single pattern of spray, for there are nozzles of all kinds that are interchangeable and also attachments that enable the pattern of spray to change in a set sequence. For the really ambitious it is even possible, although quite expensive, to install a system by which the changing spray patterns are accompanied by appropriate music. However, for most gardeners the music of the moving water itself is sufficient. The tinkling of spray on a bright reflective surface. In its simplest form a fountain can be a jet which produces half a dozen small plumes of water that gracefully return to the pool, without undue turbulence, providing the sound and movement that we all love and at the same time not totally denying us the opportunity of growing water-lilies. In warm weather this simple feature has much to commend it, for not only is it visible and audibly pleasing, but it is also much appreciated by the fish.

The same pump which provides the simple fountain, with minor additions can produce all manner of other shapes of sprays and curtains of water. The fountain plumes are very much architectural features themselves and, although transient, should be regarded in much the same light as a garden statue. The jets that produce curtains of water depend upon light for their success and can be regarded almost like flowers, for the tints and tricks of light within the spray are altered according to the season and time of day.

The traditional fountain sprays come in all manner of configurations, but the most gentle are those that are best described as volcano jets. A single central narrow column of water surrounded by smaller sprays, which produces an effect that is not unlike an exploding firework.

The inverted cone style produces a continuous circle of water like an inverted cone with the outer edge tumbling over and back into the pool; while step jets yield plumes of spray that are rather like a volcano, but one above the other, the four-step jet creating a most exquisite fountain.

There are jets that can create a pirouetting spray, a single jet surrounded by an inverted cone or ones that create bubbles and are suited to small moving water features like millstones or giving the effect of a spring in a placid pool.

Foaming fountains or geysers may not initially be thought of as possibilities for the domestic garden, but modern pumps and fountain systems have given us the opportunity of producing white water features in very small pools. Water-lilies are not a suitable proposition for such features, and a careful view should be taken as to whether fish will be happy in the turbulence created.

Large, narrow, pulsating fountain plumes are architectural features, usually operating from a simple but substantial fountain bowl. The jets are made so that the water seethes and foams, either in a turbulent twisted column, or else as a neat round-topped plume. These are essentially day-time fountains, not capable of being satisfactorily lit at night.

● *Lighting* With a moving water feature there is no need to be denied enjoyment when darkness falls, for of all the garden features it is the one that responds best to lighting. Modern sealed units can be submerged in the water focusing upon the fountain spray or lighting the area behind it. There are all kinds of colours and even a gadget that can be attached to your fountain that gives an ever-changing kaleidoscope of colours.

There are also masks and gargoyles, traditional outlets for water in the decorative garden and most useful where space is limited. So too are wall fountains, complete miniature self-contained units which in some cases can be merely hung on the wall like a picture.

For the informal water garden moving water is best presented as a waterfall. Not that waterfalls and cascades should be excluded from formal features, for some of the most famous water gardens utilize these to spectacular effect. In a formal garden their application is more rigid, the cascades being like steps and often accompanied by small fountain jets.

In the informal garden it reflects nature, trickling and tumbling down rocky crags. Often these crags are made of fibreglass or plastic and in units which can be fitted together, so the

Fig. 14 Fountains are available in many forms.

Single jet: a jet from a sculpture is traditional.

Multi-tiered: these must be in a sheltered spot.

Bell: this creates a glistening curtain of water.

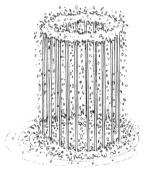

Ring: a fountain ring makes watery music.

Wall-mounted: in a confined space a mask is ideal.

Geyser: for white water use a geyser.

43

An ornamental fountain can bring movement and interest to a pool even in winter.

waterfall need not be as intimidating a prospect as one might imagine. This, together with the submersible pump which is merely placed into the pool and plugged into the electrical supply, means that the magic of moving water is within the grasp of all, whether or not you are of a practical turn of mind.

FOUNTAINS (Fig. 14)

The introduction of a fountain to the pool is a major decision, for while attractive in sight and sound it does preclude the cultivation nearby of many aquatic plants. Water-lilies, in particular, dislike the direct spray from a fountain and object to the turbulence created by the pump. So before becoming committed to a fountain it is important to look at the constraints that this will place upon the positioning and growing of plants. When a decision is taken to combine a fountain with plants, then the exact position of the fountain must be pinpointed from the outset.

Positioning

When choosing this position also bear in mind spray drift. While adjustments can always be made to the height of the jet, the positioning must be such that when the fountain is running under normal conditions, anyone passing or sitting nearby is not drenched by the spray being moved by the breeze. A considerable amount of spread needs to be allowed over the water, a factor that can only be calculated with any accuracy when the pump has been installed in its permanent position.

There are a whole range of options for fountains, varying from the simple small spray of water that does little but add the sound of moving water to the garden to the elaborate water sculpture in which the carefully created plume of water is the centre-piece of the water feature.

Installing the pump (Fig. 15)

Installation of a submersible pump either for a fountain or waterfall is simple. It is merely stood on a level plinth beneath the water. There is no reason why a small piece of paving slab should not be used. If you are creating a fountain, stand the pump level on the plinth so that the simple jet unit is just above maximum water level. Connect

▶ A terracotta pot with bubbling fountain provides a safe, easy and effective method of introducing water to the garden.

the pump to the electricity supply, the attached waterproof cable being joined to the main supply with a waterproof connector. From both the point of view of safety and convenience this should be situated beneath a paving slab. The slab can then be easily lifted during the autumn and the pump disconnected and placed in storage. It is then a simple matter to plug a pool heater into the socket for the duration of the winter.

The fountain unit

The basic fountain is produced by a simple jet unit attached to the outlet of a submersible pump. By choosing jets with different numbers and arrangements of holes, you can select you own spray pattern.

If it is inconvenient for the jet to be produced directly from the pump, or where it is required at some distance from the input, a fountain assembly unit should be used. This allows the fountain to be situated in the centre of the pool while the pump can be to one side where it is within easy reach. This installation can be used to great advantage where both a fountain and a waterfall are to be operated from the pump, with outflows at different parts of the pool.

In addition to the straightforward fountain there are a whole series of innovations that can be added in kit form. One of the most exciting in recent years has been the illuminated fountain. This is completely self-contained and creates a spectacle at night, yet doubles as an ordinary fountain during the day.

With coloured fountains it is quite possible to use a standard spray jet, but for maximum colour density a thin columnar jet is best. This is created using a special filter which has a large number of very fine holes. It is controlled by the flow adjuster directly beneath the colour changer unit.

A wide range of automatically changing spray patterns can be obtained by means of a simple device which is attached to the pump. At present it is possible to obtain as many as 18 patterns of spray in a set sequence. Each spray pattern lasts approximately 16 seconds, each complete sequence around 3½ minutes. This device can be fitted to fountains operated by either submersible or surface pumps.

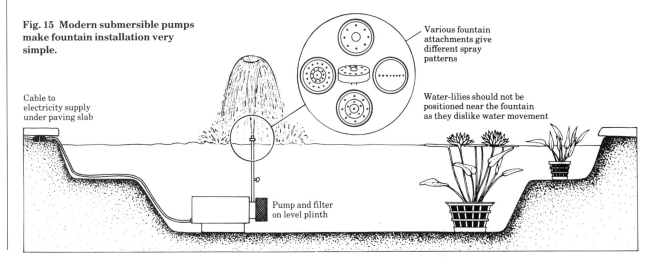

Fig. 15 Modern submersible pumps make fountain installation very simple.

Various fountain attachments give different spray patterns

Cable to electricity supply under paving slab

Water-lilies should not be positioned near the fountain as they dislike water movement

Pump and filter on level plinth

MASKS AND GARGOYLES

The range of decorative masks and gargoyles is considerable. Some require relatively elaborate plumbing arrangements, while others can be hung onto the wall rather like a mirror or a picture. There are self-contained units, or those that require the construction of a basal pool in which to collect water and from which it is re-circulated.

The traditional wall mask is of a ferocious looking animal or a mythical beast and spouts water from its mouth into a basin or pool below. The fixing of the wall mask is quite separate from the basal pool.

The basal pool must be deep enough to permit the operation of a submersible pump to re-circulate the water. If a shallow basin is required because of various aesthetic considerations, then this should be built with a drain which will permit water to flow into a hidden chamber in which the pump can be located.

This is most conveniently situated in the ground beside the basal pool. It can be easily covered with a paving slab for easy access. If this option is chosen, then the lift required to take the water up into the mask is going to be greater, for the bottom of the chamber will almost certainly be lower than the base of the pool. However, there are great advantages to having the pump hidden from view.

Traditional masks and gargoyles are fixed to a wall with a pipe running up behind them. On an existing wall it may be necessary to fasten the pipe to the wall but this does detract from the overall effect. When this is inevitable try to arrange a planting to disguise it.

If the wall has a cavity, or if you are going to build it from scratch, then there is no problem. A newly constructed wall can have a pipe incorporated into it from the start. A cavity wall can also quite simply accommodate such a pipe.

Knock a small hole through the wall on the side where the mask or gargoyle is going to be fixed at the point at which the pipe is to be connected to the spout. Take a plumb line and hold it at the centre of the hole, allowing it to hang to the base of the wall. This will give a direct alignment between the point of emergence of the pipe and where the hole should be made to thread the pipe through. Mark the wall and knock a hole through the first layer of brickwork.

In order to bring the pipe up through the wall, drop the plumb line inside the cavity. Push it through the hole at the top and permit it to fall.

· VOLUME – RATE FLOW ·			
An important factor when installing a fountain or waterfall is the amount of water movement.			
Gallons per minute	Gallons per hour	Litres per minute	Litres per hour
1	60	4.55	272.7
2	120	9.09	545.5
3	180	13.64	818.3
4	240	18.18	1,091
5	300	22.73	1,363
6	360	27.27	1,636
7	420	31.82	1,909
8	480	36.37	2,182
9	540	40.91	2,454
10	600	45.46	2,727

Unless you are extremely unlucky and it snags an internal wall tie on the way, it should fall directly in line with the basal hole. Securing the line at the top, withdraw the weight of the plumb line through the basal hole until you have sufficient to secure it to the end of the pipe which is to be attached to the mask and the pump. By pulling the line back up, the pipe will be drawn through the wall cavity for securing to the mask or gargoyle. This will cover the hole in the upper wall and the lower hole will be part of the back wall of the pool into which the pipe is secured.

A combination of features that employ moving water – a lion mask spouts into a gentle cascade.

WATERFALLS

Waterfalls are lovely additions to the garden pool, adding movement and sound which can be happily accommodated in either a formal or informal feature.

They are easiest to place in the informal or natural garden. Ideally the terrain is such that if water were to be seen it would be expected to tumble about. The site must either be on a slope or be re-graded so that there are slopes or banks.

In nature waterfalls can be divided into two: those that are vigorous, tumbling and rushing – often the legacy of snow-melt higher upstream – or alternatively permanent trickling, twinkling ribbons of water over very worn algae-covered rock. In the garden each has role to play.

The waterfalls that crash rather than tinkle can be incorporated into a strong formal scheme. Here there need be no effort made to simulate nature. In a garden a bold rushing waterfall is making a statement.

What the statement might be is a matter of conjecture, but it fits hand in glove with bold angles and strong shapes. It can be raw and informal, almost like a chute rather than a cascade, throwing water strongly from one pool to another. Here plants play second fiddle to the movement of water, the feature becoming almost like a moving sculpture in an unnatural but artistic seting. Lighting can play an important role, especially coloured lights directed at the water once it has left the chute.

Formal waterfalls can be useful in transferring water from one raised pool to another when built side by side. This is more meaningful than a main pool with water cascading and re-circulating. The pools that benefit from visual linking may not require their water moved, but visually it is appealing.

A formal waterfall tumbling into an informal pool defies design convention, but is effective nonetheless.

Natural waterfalls can either be of the kind that sparkle amongst overhanging plants, or provide a moving ribbon of light through a rocky mountain-like terrain. The heavily planted waterfall is only appropriate when you unexpectedly come upon it. There is no way in which it can form a focal point or feature. It should provide the experience of quiet reflectiveness and is therefore best placed in a secret corner of the garden where when the visitor comes upon it, he has to retrace his steps to retreat.

Waterfall installation

The most frequently installed waterfall is constructed of pre-formed fibreglass, PVC or plastic units comprising a header pool and cascade drops. These are available in different finishes, from textured rock to grit and pebble dash. Each is capable of accumulating micro flora such as algae and after a period of time will begin to blend with its surroundings and look completely natural (Fig. 16).

Before making a final selection of a pre-formed cascade, be sure that it is in proportion to your water feature. Nobody can tell you exactly how it should appear, but a large pool with a waterfall that dribbles into it or a small pool with a tumbling rushing cascade are each out of keeping. At the same time check that there is ample provision to disguise the hosepipe carrying the water to the header pool in the area where the waterfall is proposed.

When installing the waterfall, lay out the units approximately where they are to be placed, sprinkling sand around each to provide a rough guide for digging. Dig out separate pockets to accommodate each unit and the header pool. Start with the lower unit, making sure that the lip protrudes over the edge of the pool. Bed each unit in sand, where necessary providing additional support with large stones or bricks. These should be used as supports in areas where the unit may twist if just resting on sand. To some extent these points will be determined by the lie of the land, the more support that is required, the greater the need for a brick or large stone.

When complete the unit should rest firmly on a sand bed, receiving support for its entire length.

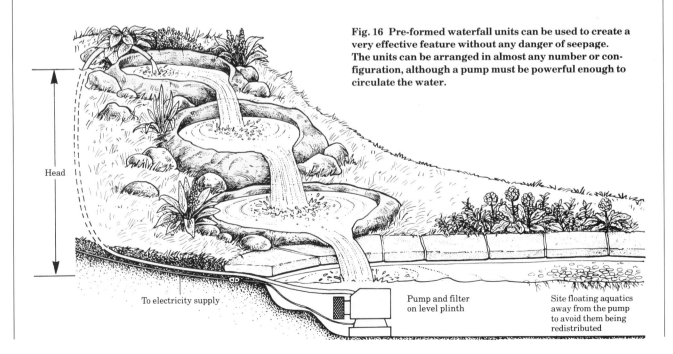

Fig. 16 Pre-formed waterfall units can be used to create a very effective feature without any danger of seepage. The units can be arranged in almost any number or configuration, although a pump must be powerful enough to circulate the water.

Head

To electricity supply

Pump and filter on level plinth

Site floating aquatics away from the pump to avoid them being redistributed

Check carefully with a spirit level to see whether it is level from side to side. This is vital if the effect of water is to be realistic and natural looking. Fill around the sides with soil, giving an effect as far as possible of the waterfall having been worn away in the ground rather than placed upon it. Nearby planting will do much to help disguise the edges.

During construction ensure that each pouring lip overlaps the next. Take the delivery hose and position it at the edge of the header pool. Some header pools have a small groove cut into them which accommodates the hose without interfering with the surroundings of the feature. This makes it easier to disguise the water source with rocks. The water should ideally appear as if emerging from a spring rather than just pouring into the header pool.

OTHER WATER FEATURES

Millstones

These are very fashionable nowadays and are wonderful for turning into water features. It is not necessary to own one of the real heavy stone kinds as there are manufacturers who produce fake millstones in high quality fibreglass. Once well established and with a little algal deposit on it, an artificial millstone can look like the real thing, for most are finished with a dusting of sand. The big advantage for the water gardener is that they are light and relatively easy to move about.

A millstone fountain provides an opportunity for a very safe water feature. The sort of feature which can be happily associated with small children, for the water is pumped up through the centre of the millstone, is dissipated across the top and disappears through the surrounding cobbles into a container below (Fig. 17).

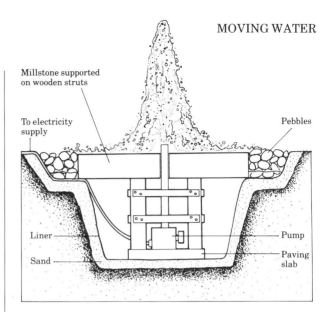

Millstone supported on wooden struts

To electricity supply

Pebbles

Liner

Pump

Sand

Paving slab

Fig. 17 A millstone water feature is both a safe and effective way of bringing moving water into the garden.

A pebble fountain is constructed in a similar way, The fountain jet being arranged so that it is level with the top of the layer of cobbles. The jet can be a simple bubbler, or alternatively a bell fountain or small geyser. Providing that it is not too violent it is really a matter of personal choice as to what height and configuration your pebble fountain spray takes.

Rills and streams

Few gardeners are fortunate enough to possess a natural rill or stream. Most have to create their own artificially. While this may seem to be a disadvantage at first sight, at least there is some control over a feature that has been artificially contrived. One of the greatest hazards of a natural stream is the unpredictable nature of its flow. It may be a reliable and consistent source of water during spring and summer, but it is likely to become an uncontrollable raging torrent during the winter, especially after the melting of any snow.

◀ The careful placing of various-shaped rocks can be used to influence the flow and effect of tumbling waters.

▶ The two faces of water in the garden – a fast-flowing cascade contrasting with the serene stillness of a pool.

Natural streams and rills

Despite reservations about the variability of the quantity of water at different seasons, natural streams and rills are generally a bonus. A stream that has been running in the same place for many years is likely to have an attractive stony bottom which would be almost impossible to recreate artificially. It will also have its complement of wildlife which will not just circulate between stream and pool as with the artificial construction, but from upstream too. A natural stream will have its own ecology which is most attractive to the wildlife gardener.

Streams and rills place responsibilities upon their owners for they are taking water from land above and depositing it on someone else's land below. During the passage through a property the flow of the stream must not be interfered with. The only safe and legal way the flow of a natural stream may be checked or diverted slightly is by the addition of stepping stones.

● *Erosion* Even quite small natural streams can suffer from erosion. Generally this occurs during winter when the water level may rise substantially. It is most frequent near a bend, for this diverts the main water current from the centre and can lead to erosion by scouring or undermining the base of the bank so that the top subsides. Sheet erosion of the top soil can also occur, but not only near bends.

If erosion is likely to be a serious problem then an artificial method of protection is necessary. Wood is the easiest material to work with and the most acceptable in the garden. Drive strong stakes into the edge of the stream bed where the erosion is taking place. They should be placed 90 cm (3 ft) apart and rough planks of wood placed on the inside, the eroded area now being protected from the stream and filled with soil.

> · HANDY TIP ·
>
> If preparing a natural stream for planting, do not physically remove the native vegetation. Spray it with a glyphosate-based weedkiller and allow the dying roots to hold the soil together while the new plants become established. This is most effective against soil erosion.

If erosion is not too severe, but more irritating, then much can be done with the strategic placement of plants along the stream margin. Plant on the outside of any bend, allowing the inside to be free from plants.

Artificial streams

It is rarely possible to create a natural-bottomed stream artificially which will function without losing large amounts of water. An artificially constructed stream, whether made from a pool liner or pre-formed sections is infinitely better. With the careful placing of stones or gravel on the stream bed and planting naturally right up to the edge, most artificial streams can be disguised successfully.

● *Lining a stream* The method of constructing a stream using a liner is broadly similar to that for a pool constructed of the same material (see pages 23–4).

Excavate the stream in the final shape and size required. It should link from a header pool to the main pool, the water being re-circulated by a submersible pump in the same way as described for a waterfall. The stream bed should slope, but not acutely. Movement in the water is more effectively created by the careful placement of stones than the awkward configuration of an excavation.

Once satisfied with the excavation, scour it for sticks, stones or any sharp objects that may puncture the liner. Lay fleece or a layer of sand evenly across the bottom and up the sides of the stream.

Spread the liner over the stream bed and secure it to the edges with stones, or else by tucking it beneath the soil. Where soil and liner meet should always be above the maximum water line or else the stream water will soak away into the surrounding soil. A liner-made stream can be left untouched, but the best visual effect results from covering the stream bed with stones or cobbles and permitting plants to grow in pockets of soil along its edge.

Fig. 18 Building a stream is simple with modern materials.

● *Pre-formed streams* In recent years prefabricated streams with curves and twists have become increasingly available. They fasten together in a similar manner to the track of a toy train set.

The excavation for a pre-formed stream should be slightly larger than the plastic or fibreglass shapes. Place the stream sections on the ground and run a line of sand around the shape to give you an idea of the area to dig out. Once the excavation is complete spread sand over the floor so that the stream sections can be rested level on the soft base. Backfill around with soil ensuring that each section is very securely bedded (Fig. 18).

Some pre-formed streams have special height adjuster panels that enable compensations in levels to be achieved on sloping sites. Each 1.5 m (5 ft) of length can be bridged by a fall of about

(a) Use a spirit level on a plank of wood to check that the sides of the excavation are level.

(b) Start at the bottom of the stream and overlap successive pre-formed units.

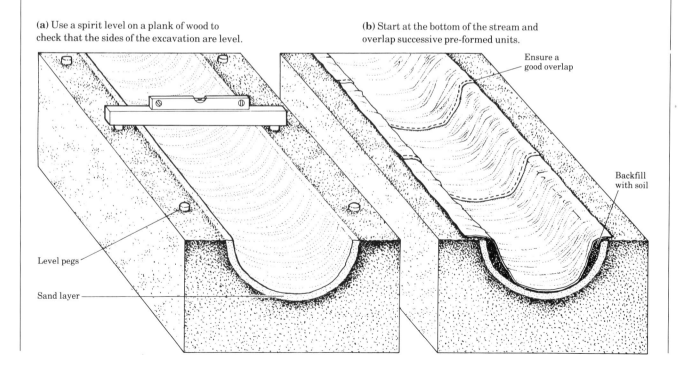

Ensure a good overlap

Backfill with soil

Level pegs

Sand layer

30 cm (12 in). When the circulation pump is switched off the water level is always maintained in the individual stream components which are sealed off from one another by the height adjustment. Only surplus water runs away.

Lighting a water feature

Water features can be greatly enhanced by lighting. Nowadays there is a whole range of options which can be used to illuminate the water garden from both beneath the water and around the outside.

The most spectacular effects are created from lighting beneath the water. Underwater lighting is usually manufactured as a single spotlight, but it is often possible to purchase a unit with two or three lights secured together. This is ideal for the larger fountain or waterfall.

The spotlight is normally of white light, the colours being provided by clip-on lenses of different colours. This is static lighting which provides a single colour, but it is now also possible to have a smaller lighting unit which attaches to the pump and fountain outlet with a series of colours. As the pump operates, this colour changer rotates and presents a series of different coloured fountain sprays.

The colour changer does not have the versatility of ordinary spotlights which can be placed at any point in the pool and with a little experimentation can be made to produce quite remarkable effects. They can be focused upon fountain or waterfall or used to light up the depths of the pool the graceful but gloomy figures of the fish.

◀ An artificial stream can be made to appear quite natural by the skilful planting of moisture-loving plants.

▶ Paving slabs provide a safe and simple method of crossing a stream and do not intrude upon this informal setting.

· 4 ·
Plants and Planting

Creating and maintaining a balance with careful planting is essential if the pool is to be a permanent success. Think of the pool as a miniature underwater world where plants and livestock depend upon one another for their continued existence. In order to create a balance from the outset it is essential that submerged plants are introduced at the rate of one bunch to every 0.093 sq m (1 sq ft) of surface area of the pool and that between one third and a half of the surface area of the pool is covered with floating foliage. This need not necessarily be free-floating plants, for water-lilies and other deep water aquatics can be just as effective at providing cover with their floating leaves.

Planting (Fig. 19)

While some gardeners advocate planting directly into soil on the pool floor, the majority agree that pool management is so much better if aquatic plants are restricted to a container. For water-lilies, deep water aquatics and marginal plants the specially manufactured plastic lattice-work aquatic planting containers are the most suitable. These are of stable construction and have lattice-work sides which permit gaseous exchange between water and roots. It is advisable to line them with hessian before planting to prevent soil spillage into the water. Use a proper aquatic planting compost or a good heavy garden soil which is devoid of any twigs, debris or organic matter which may pollute the water. Plant firmly, water well and then top dress the compost with fine gravel to prevent the fish from stirring it up when they poke around. Submerged plants must be planted so that the lead weights are buried, but floating aquatics are merely tossed on to the surface of the water. All aquatic plants are best planted in spring, although the season extends until mid-summer.

DEEP WATER AQUATICS

Water-lilies (*Nymphaea* varieties)

Water-lilies inhabit the deeper areas of the pool producing floating foliage and blossoms of great beauty. Most gardeners grow water-lilies in containers for convenience, but in large natural waterscapes they are planted directly into the pool floor. The figures in parentheses following each variety indicate the depth at which that variety will grow best. For the most part the surface spread of the foliage will be between one and one and a half times the depth at which the water-lily is growing. For example, a plant that is recommended as growing in 60 cm (2 ft) of water is likely to have a spread of between 60–90 cm (2–3 ft) (Fig. 20).

Nymphaea 'Attraction'. A lovely plant for deeper water where it can be allowed to develop to its full potential. Immense garnet-red flowers, up to 23 cm (9 in) across, attractively flecked with white. Rich mahogany stamens with conspicuous yellow tips. Off-white sepals with a rosy flush. Large green leaves. 90 cm–1.2 m (3–4 ft).

N. 'Aurora'. One of the finest water-lilies for tub culture. It produces creamy coloured flower buds which open yellow and then pass through orange to blood red. Mottled purplish and olive-green foliage. 30–45 cm (1–1½ ft).

N. 'Conqueror'. Crimson cup-shaped blossoms with white flecks and flakes that may attain 15 cm (6 in) across. Central clusters of bright yellow stamens. Young foliage purple but turning green as it matures. 60–75 cm (2–2½ ft).

N. 'Escarboucle'. One of the best known and larger growing water-lilies. In the average garden pool it is impossible to do it justice. Large fragrant crimson flowers up to 30 cm (12 in) across with bright yellow stamens. Enormous deep green leaves. 90 cm–1.8 m (3–6 ft).

N. 'Froebelii'. A popular red water-lily for the smaller pool. Handsome deep blood red blossoms with bright orange stamens are produced amongst dull purplish-green leaves. 45–60 cm (1½–2 ft).

N. 'Gloire de Temple-sur-Lot'. Regarded by many as the choicest of water-lilies, this variety has delicately incurved petals of rosy pink in fully double array. As the blossoms fade they turn pale pink. Bright yellow stamens. Leaves large and plain green. 60–90 cm (2–3 ft).

N. 'Gonnère'. Some gardeners know this plant as 'Crystal White', a fully double pure white water-lily with distinctive bright green sepals. Very rounded pea-green leaves amongst which the blossoms sit like floating snowballs. 60–75 cm (2–2½ ft).

N. 'James Brydon'. Large crimson peony-shaped flowers amongst dark purplish-green leaves which are flecked with maroon. 45–90 cm (1½–3 ft).

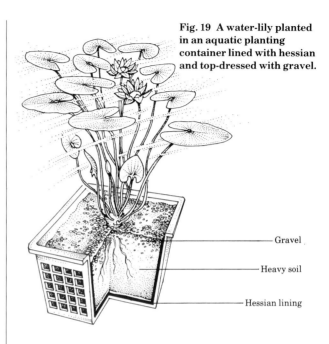

Fig. 19 A water-lily planted in an aquatic planting container lined with hessian and top-dressed with gravel.

Gravel

Heavy soil

Hessian lining

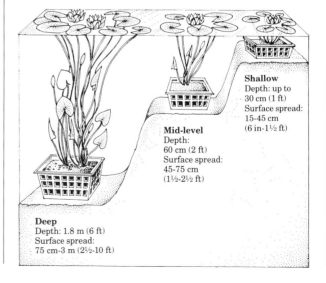

Fig. 20 There are three main planting depths for different varieties of water-lily.

Shallow
Depth: up to 30 cm (1 ft)
Surface spread: 15-45 cm (6 in-1½ ft)

Mid-level
Depth: 60 cm (2 ft)
Surface spread: 45-75 cm (1½-2½ ft)

Deep
Depth: 1.8 m (6 ft)
Surface spread: 75 cm-3 m (2½-10 ft)

Laydekeri hybrids These are small-growing hybrids which are excellent for tub culture or for growing in smaller pools. All grow in as little as 30 cm (12 in) of water, although they will not come to any harm in up to 60 cm (2 ft).

N. laydekeri 'Alba'. Pure white blossoms with yellow stamens and an unusual tea fragrance. Plain green leaves.

N. laydekeri 'Fulgens'. Fragrant bright crimson flowers with reddish stamens. Dark green foliage, purple beneath.

N. laydekeri 'Purpurata'. Rich deep red blossoms with bright orange stamens. The leaves are

small, plain green with occasional splashes of black or maroon, undersides purple.

Marliacea hybrids include *N. marliacea* 'Albida', unquestionably the best known and most widely cultivated white water-lily. Scented blossoms some 15 cm (6 in) across held just above the water. The reverse of the petals sometimes shows a pink flush. Deep green leaves with purplish undersides. 45–90 cm (1½–3 ft).

N. marliacea 'Carnea'. One of the most popular large-growing pink-flowered water-lilies. The blossoms can be up to 20 cm (8 in) across, have a vanilla fragrance and conspicuous central clusters of bright golden stamens. Juvenile foliage is purplish but turns dark green with age. For the first year after planting white flowers are often produced. 60 cm–1.5 m (2–5 ft).

N. marliacea 'Chromatella'. Canary-yellow flowers up to 15 cm (6 in) across, the outer petals and sepals often showing a pinkish flush. Large olive-green leaves boldly splashed in maroon and bronze. 45–75 cm (1½–2½ ft).

N. odorata 'Firecrest'. Deep red-pink flowers with distinctive red-tipped stamens. Dark green leaves with a strong purplish caste. 45–90 cm (1½–3½ ft).

Pygmaea hybrids The pygmy water-lilies are capable of growing happily in as little as 15 cm (6 in) of water. They are complete miniature replicas of the popular water-lilies rather than dwarf forms.

N. pygmaea 'Alba'. The smallest water-lily, each blossom being no more than 2–5 cm (1–2 in) across. The foliage is tiny, more or less oval and dark green with purple undersides. Up to 30 cm (12 in).

◀ The beautiful *Nymphaea* 'Leopardess' is a tropical water-lily but it can be grown successfully in areas that have warm summers.

Nymphaea marliacea
'Albida' is one of the most beautiful and versatile white-flowered water-lilies for the average pool.

N. pygmaea 'Helvola'. The most free-flowering and reliable of the pygmy water-lilies. Canary-yellow flowers with orange stamens amongst olive-green leaves that are heavily mottled with purple and brown.

N. pygmaea 'Rubis'. A little beauty, but a shy flowerer. Blood red blossoms with bright orange stamens. Tiny purplish-green leaves with reddish undersides.

· WATER-LILY PESTS AND DISEASES·		
Name	*Description*	*Control*
Water-lily aphis	Attacks water-lilies, but also other succulent plants; small black insects which cover the foliage.	Winter wash nearby plum and cherry trees to kill over-wintering eggs; wash aphis into the water with a jet of water from a hosepipe; the fish will soon clear them up.
Water-lily beetle	Water-lily leaves and flowers are torn and shredded, only the veins remaining; the beetle grub which causes the damage is black and shiny.	Good poolside maintenance in winter is essential to prevent hibernation by the pool; dislodging the pests with a jet of water and allowing the fish to clear them up is the only effective summer control.
Water-lily leaf spots	Brown spots or splashes on the foliage that eventually rot.	Remove afflicted leaves as soon as they are noticed to prevent spread of disease.
Water-lily crown rot	The crowns decompose in a brown rotting mass and the leaves become detached.	No cure; remove plants and burn; thoroughly clean the pool and disinfect.

N. 'Rose Arey'. One of the best fragrant water-lilies, the star-like blossoms imparting a rich aroma of aniseed. Rose-pink petals and bright yellow stamens. Young foliage crimson, adult leaves green with a reddish tinge. 45–75 cm (1½–2½ ft).

N. 'Virginalis'. Pure white semi-double blossoms with yellow stamens and pink flushed sepals. Plain green leaves flushed with purple. 45–75 cm (1½–2½ ft).

N. 'William Falconer'. Blood-red flowers with yellow stamens. Olive-green leaves which are purple when young. 45–75 cm (1½–2½ ft).

Other deep water aquatics

In addition to water-lilies there are a number of other aquatic plants which can be grown in the deeper parts of the pool. These require exactly the same cultural treatment as water-lilies, although many are more tolerant of adverse conditions such as moving water and partial shade. The figures in brackets are the depths of water between which each species will grow successfully.

Aponogeton distachyos (water hawthorn). A most reliable plant. Almost evergreen and capable of providing a continuous display of blossoms from early spring until autumn. The sweetly scented white flowers are forked and bear a double row of bract-like organs at the base of which are clusters of jet-black stamens. Readily increased by division in the spring, although it will often seed itself freely. 30–90 cm (1–3 ft).

Nuphar lutea (yellow pond-lily). A large coarse plant which requires a lot of room. Small bottle-shaped yellow flowers are produced for much of the summer amongst masses of leathery green leaves reminiscent of those of a water-lily (Fig. 21). Readily propagated by division in early spring. 30 cm–2.4m (1–8 ft).

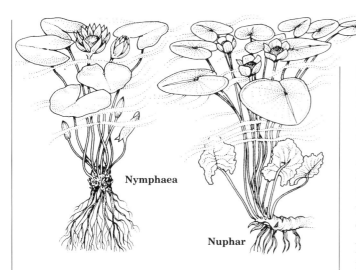

Nymphaea

Nuphar

Fig. 21 Nymphaeas are the true water-lilies, Nuphars are pond lilies and too vigorous for most pools.

Nymphoides peltata (water fringe). This provides a wonderful display of delicately fringed buttercup-like flowers during late summer amongst handsome green and brown mottled foliage. Although *Nymphoides* can be raised from seed, they are more usually increased from spring and summer divisions of the scrambling rootstock. 30–75 cm (1–2½ ft).

Orontium aquaticum (golden club). A very adaptable plant providing a striking display of yellow and white pencil-like flowers during late spring. These stand clear of the water amongst narrow waxy glaucous foliage. Can be increased easily from seed provided it is sown when it is still green.

MARGINAL AQUATIC PLANTS (Fig. 22)

It is these plants which grow around the edge of a pool, preferring mud or just a few inches of water, but being equally capable of tolerating periodic inundation. Although most adaptable and decorative, marginal aquatics contribute little to the balance of the water environment. All the marginal aquatic plants described here will tolerate up to about 15 cm (6 in) of water cover, although some will grow more successfully in shallower water.

Alisma plantago-aquatica (water plantain). An easy-going plant with attractive oval foliage and in summer loose pyramidal panicles of pink and white flowers. Increased by seed or division during spring. 45–75 cm (1½–2½ ft).

Butomus umbellatus (flowering rush). Spreading umbels of dainty rose-pink flowers on stout erect flower stems which ascend through masses of narrow twisted foliage during late summer. Increased by collecting the small bulbils which appear in the basal axils of the leaves and pushing them into mud just beneath the water. 60–90 cm (2–3 ft).

Calla palustris (bog arum). A most useful plant for disguising the edge of the pool. It spreads by means of stout creeping rhizomes which are clothed in handsome glossy, heart-shaped foliage. The small white flowers are rather like miniature florists' arums, but not so beautifully sculptured. They are followed by spikes of bright red berries which contain seeds that germinate freely if sown immediately. 15–60 cm (6–12 in).

Caltha palustris (marsh marigold). A familiar swamp plant which during spring is garlanded with waxy blossoms of intense golden-yellow. There is also a fully double form with bright yellow blossoms, rather like those of a pompon dahlia, on a compact plant with handsome dark green glossy foliage. The single marsh marigold can be increased by seed sown immediately it ripens or by spring division of the crowns. The double form can only be increased by division. 30–75 cm (1–2½ ft).

Iris varieties. The truly acquatic irises are amongst the most colourful marginal subjects.

Iris laevigata. A lovely blue iris which has given rise to innumerable attractive hybrids. Amongst the best are the violet and white 'Colchesteri', white 'Alba' and soft pink 'Rose Queen'. There is also a fine variegated foliage kind known variously as 'Variegata' or 'Elegantissima'. All flower during summer and are best divided immediately flowering is over. 75–90 cm (1½–3 ft).

I. pseudacorus (yellow flag). A large vigorous plant that until recent times did not figure largely as a marginal plant in the garden pool. The recent trend towards wildlife ponds has ensured its future. For garden decoration choose the soft primrose variety *bastardii* or bright golden yellow 'Golden Queen'. The most spectacular is the variegated foliage cultivar 'Variegata', although this rarely attains the height of the other kinds. Increased by division in summer immediately after flowering. 75–1.35 cm (2½–4½ ft).

I. versicolor. Strong violet-blue flowers veined with purple and splashed gold. The variety 'Kermesina' is even more lovely, having blooms of deep velvety plum with similar distinctive markings. Plain green sword-like leaves. Increased by division during summer directly after flowering.

Mentha aquatica (water mint). This strongly aromatic plant enjoys shallow water or mud at the poolside and when growing happily produces dense terminal whorls of lilac pink flowers during late summer amidst an abundance of hairy greyish-green foliage. Easily increased by summer cuttings or division during early spring. 23–45 cm (9 in–1½ ft).

Menyanthes trifoliata (bog bean). A very distinctive plant for shallow water. It bears decorative white fringed flowers during late spring above dark green trifoliate leaves, much like those of a broad bean. If the creeping stem is chopped into sections, each with a root attached, these will rapidly develop into small plants. 23–30 cm (9–12 in).

Myosotis scorpioides (water forget-me-not). During early summer this charming little plant is smothered in sky-blue flowers that are almost identical to those of the familiar bedding forget-me-not. An improved form called 'Semperflorens' is even lovelier, producing fewer leaves and being more compact. Seed raising is the most usual means of propagation. Occasionally seed-raised

▼ *Iris laevigata*
'Colchesteri' is one of the finest marginal aquatics. It grows in damp conditions or in several inches of water.

▶ Ferns, hostas, candelabra primulas and irises associate happily together in this bog garden.

Fig. 22 Marginal aquatics.

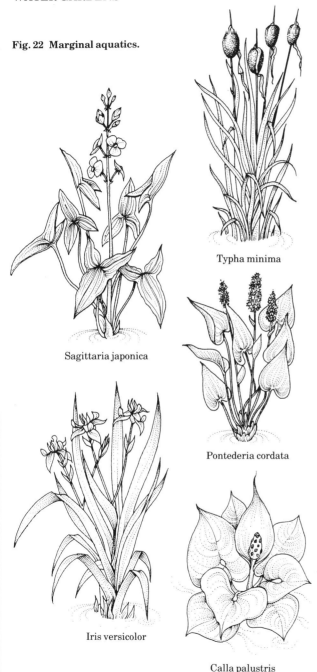

Typha minima

Sagittaria japonica

Pontederia cordata

Iris versicolor

Calla palustris

plants will yield an attractive white-flowered individual. 15–23 cm (6–9 in).

Pontederia cordata (pickerel). A plant of noble proportions, producing numerous stems each consisting of an oval or lance-like shiny green leaf and a leafy bract from which a spike of soft blue flowers emerges during late summer. Propagation is by division of the rootstocks in early spring. 45–90 cm (1½–3 ft).

Sagittaria japonica (arrowhead). A handsome plant with arrow-shaped foliage from which tiered spikes of white-petalled flowers are produced during summer. There is also a beautiful fully double-flowered form called 'Flore-Pleno'. *Sagittaria* grows from large winter buds which look rather like bulbs and these can be lifted and redistributed in the spring. 45–60 cm (1½–2 ft).

Scirpus lacustris (bulrush). The true bulrush produces stiff dark green needle-like leaves from short hardy creeping rhizomes and during summer produces pendant tassels of crowded reddish-brown flowers. Increased by spring division. 60 cm–1.2 m (2–4 ft).

S. tabernaemontanii 'Zebrinus' (zebra rush). A popular mutant in which the stems are alternately barred with green and white. It does best when allowed to colonize very shallow water. Propagation by late spring division. 90 cm (3 ft).

Typha angustifolia (narrow-leafed reedmace). A very impressive plant for the larger pool with its bold poker-like seed heads. The narrow-leafed cousin of the common reedmace.

T. minima. This splendid little plant produces masses of short fat brown flower spikes amongst dark green grassy foliage. Can be successfully accommodated in the tiniest pool. Increased by division during early spring. 30–45 cm (1–1½ ft).

· HANDY TIP ·

In deep water or gloomy conditions grow the hornwort (*Ceratophyllum demersum*). This submerged aquatic does not root, but remains just beneath the surface of the water irrespective of its depth.

Veronica beccabunga (brooklime). The brooklime has many uses, being particularly valuable for climbing out of the water and masking the area where pool meets land. During summer its dark green glossy foliage is sprinkled with tiny blue and white flowers. Propagation, which should be undertaken annually in the spring, is by short stem cuttings pushed into the mud or a tray of wet soil. 15–23 cm (6–9 in).

SUBMERGED PLANTS

Submerged aquatic plants play a vital role in maintaining water clarity. It is not the oxygen that they produce which is the key, although this is obviously of great benefit to other aquatic life, it is the fact that they compete with slimes and algae for dissolved mineral salts in the water. Obviously if sufficient competition is provided, then the more primitive water-discolouring plants like algae die out.

To ensure reasonable clarity from the outset, submerged aquatics should be planted at a density of one bunch to every 0.093 sq m (1 sq ft) of surface area. This is calculated as being the total pool area excluding that occupied by the marginal shelves.

That is not to say that they should be distributed checkerboard style across the floor of the pool, it is the total volume of plant material that is introduced that is important. Bunches may be planted in two or three strategically placed containers and be equally effective and much easier to manage.

Very few submerged plants are sold as growing plants, the majority are purchased as bunches of cuttings. These are generally young vigorous growths which are held together by a small strip of lead. Once introduced to the water they rapidly initiate roots and grow away.

· SUBMERGED PLANTS FOR SPECIAL PURPOSES ·

Name	Description	Use
Callitriche platycarpa (starwort)	A bright green cress-like plant.	A fine green food for fish; provides a safe haven for aquatic insect life.
Eleocharis acicularis (hairgrass)	Creeping underwater colonies of grass-like foliage; sold as a plant, not as a bunch of cuttings.	Ideal for carpeting the floor of small pools and tubs.
Fontinalis antipyretica (willow moss)	Dark olive-green, thick mossy foliage.	A perfect plant for fish spawning; grows well in fast-moving water.
Myriophyllum verticillatum (whorled milfoil)	Bright green needle-like foliage carried in dense whorls on long stems.	A good plant for fish to spawn into.
Potomogeton crispus (curled pondweed)	Dark bronze-green crinkly foliage not unlike seaweed; small spikes of crimson and cream flowers.	One of the most decorative submerged aquatics.
Ranunculus aquatilis (water crowfoot)	Dense, fine green submerged foliage, occasional surface leaves and bright white and yellow flowers.	Very decorative and an excellent plant for fish spawning.

Elodea canadensis (Canadian pond weed). One of the most versatile and successful submerged plants. Small dark green, lance-like leaves carried in dense whorls along extensive branching stems.

Hottonia palustris (water violet). Probably the finest hardy submerged aquatic, but one of the most fickle. A beautiful plant with large whorls of bright green foliage and spikes of whitish or lilac-tinted blossoms. Rarely does this succeed when introduced to a newly established pool. *Hottonia* produces turions of winter buds which ensure its distribution to other parts of the pool where the following season it may reappear unexpectedly. Readily increased from summer stem cuttings.

Lagarosiphon major. Probably the best known and most widely planted submerged aquatic. The common fish weed of the pet shop where it is usually sold under its better known name, *Elodea crispa*. Long, trailing dark green stems clothed in dense whorls of dark green crispy foliage. Easily increased from cuttings taken at any time during the active growing season.

Myriophyllum spicatum (spiked milfoil). A favourite plant of the fish fancier. Handsome, much-divided foliage on long slender stems that provides an excellent spawning ground for gold-fish. The whorls of tiny leaflets are coppery-green in the spring, but turn bronze as the summer progresses. As the stems reach the surface of the water they push up tiny crimson and yellow flower spikes. Increased by stem cuttings at any time in the growing season before flower buds are seen.

◀ A distinctly oriental flavour can be achieved by planting hostas, astilbes and variegated iris in association with the Japanese maple.

FLOATING AQUATICS (Fig. 23)

It is free-floating aquatic plants that make a major contribution to the maintenance of a correct balance within the pool. Along with the floating foliage of deep water aquatics they reduce the amount of sunlight that falls directly into the water, thereby making it difficult for algae to survive. Floating aquatics derive their nourishment directly from the water. They use the available mineral salts, working alongside the submerged plants to deprive suspended algae of any substance.

Floating aquatics do not require planting, just placing on the water surface water. As the majority of floating plants reproduce freely by division of runners it is difficult to give a predictable spread. All can be maintained at the density desired merely by netting or removing by hand.

Azolla caroliniana (fairy moss). A small floating fern which congregates in dense but controllable masses. The individual plantlets are of a bluish-green colour, somewhat lacy in appearance and in excessive light or at the approach of autumn turn purplish-red.

Eichhornia crassipes (water hyacinth). A tender aquatic which can spend the summer outside in cooler areas. Although not frost hardy and only flowering sparingly in the open in cool districts, most gardeners like to grow it for its extraordinary foliage. This is very handsome, dark glossy green and rather flattened, but with inflated bases that are honeycombed inside to give the plant buoyancy. From amongst the strange cluster of balloon-type foliage emerge strong spikes of blue and lilac orchid-like blossoms, each with a bright peacock eye. Reproduces freely from runners during the summer months, the young plantlets being easy to overwinter in shallow bowls of mud in a warm place in cold districts.

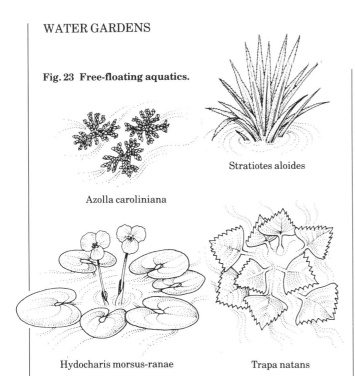

Fig. 23 Free-floating aquatics.

Stratiotes aloides

Azolla caroliniana

Hydocharis morsus-ranae

Trapa natans

Hydrocharis morsus-ranae (frogbit). Not unlike a tiny water-lily, although it is not related. Neat rosettes of small, dull green, kidney-shaped leaves from which simple three-petalled white flowers with bright yellow centres are produced.

Like most floating aquatics the frogbit forms winter buds or turions which sink to the bottom of the pool. These disappear during early autumn and reappear in late spring when the water temperature starts to rise.

Stratiotes aloides (water soldier). A very unusual floating aquatic with foliage which is reminiscent of a pineapple top. The leaves are dark olive-green, spiky and carried in neat rosettes which float at, or just above, the surface of the water. Creamy-white papery flowers are produced in the axils of the leaves. A persistent plant that reproduces freely from runners.

Trapa natans (water chestnut). Although this is technically an annual plant, once introduced to a pool it becomes a perennial in all but name. Each plant is a neat rosette of dark green floating rhomboidal foliage from which emerge delicate white blossoms. As the summer wears on hard black spiny nuts or seeds are produced which fall to the bottom of the pool for the winter months, germinating the following spring and re-appearing on the surface of the water.

BOG PLANTS

It is difficult to draw a line between bog and marginal plants, but most gardeners accept that those plants which prosper in standing water are marginal plants, while the ones that require very wet conditions, but will not tolerate long periods of inundation are bog plants. A bog is a very wet peripheral area of the water garden (Fig. 24) while the margins refer to the shallows of the pool.

Astilbe hybrids (false goat's beard). The astilbes are a wide-ranging group of perennials with handsome feathery plumes of flowers produced above bold clumps of attractive divided green foliage. All flower from mid- to late summer. Amongst the more popular hybrids are 'White Gloria', the salmon-pink 'Peach Blossom' and bright crimson 'Fanal'. All are easily increased by division of the coarse woody rootstock during winter or early spring. 60 cm–1.2 m (2–4 ft).

Filipendula ulmaria (meadow sweet). Frothy spires of creamy-white blossoms are produced during summer above handsome deeply-cut dark green foliage. The double form is the most satisfactory to grow for flowers, while the golden-leafed 'Aurea' has the most striking foliage. Increase by division during winter or early spring. 60 cm–1.5 m (2–5 ft).

Hosta (plantain lily). Hostas are amongst the most valuable foliage plants for the bog garden and waterside planting.

Hosta glauca. One of the largest of the plantain lilies. Big, bold glaucous heart-shaped leaves up to 15 cm (6 in) wide and often twice as long make an attractive summer feature. Slender flower spike support pendant, dull white bell-like blossoms. The cultivar 'Robusta' is larger still and often planted as a focal point. Easily increased by division in the spring just as the shoots are emerging. 30–60 cm (1–2 ft).

H. lancifolia. A green foliage species with long lance-shaped leaves which during mid-summer produces erect sprays of lilac blossoms. The cultivar 'Fortis' is larger in every respect, 'Aurea' has lovely golden foliage and the hybrid 'Thomas Hogg' which boasts *H. lancifolia* in its parentage, has plain green leaves with a bold white marginal band. Propagated by spring division. 30–60 cm (1–2 ft).

H. undulata medio-variegata. The most popular variegated plantain lily. Brightly coloured cream, green and white leaves which are somewhat twisted and undulated. If it shows signs of flowering, remove the buds as these detract from the beauty of the plant. Increase by spring division. 30 cm (12 in).

Iris varieties. Bog garden irises are reliable and colourful additions to moist areas, providing lasting mid-summer interest.

Iris kaempferi (Japanese clematis-flowered iris). This beautiful swamp iris has tufts of broad grassy foliage surmounted by exotic clematis-like flowers. Amongst the best varieties are 'Blue Heaven' with rich purple-blue velvety petals marked with yellow, the fully double pale rose-lavender 'Landscape at Dawn' and deep violet 'Mandarin'. There is also a very attractive cream and green-variegated foliage cultivar called 'Variegata' which has the added bonus of small deep violet-blue flowers. All *I. kaempferi* varieties flower during mid-summer. Named varieties are increased by division immediately after flowering. Good mixed strains can be raised from seed sown during early spring. Unlike the majority of other irises, the clematis-flowered varieties must have an acid soil. 45–75 cm (1½–2½ ft).

I. sibirica (Siberian iris). Easy-going irises with smaller blossoms than *I. kaempferi* and narrower grassy leaves. Tolerant of almost any moist soil conditions. The common species has pale blue flowers and is a rather subdued plant, but its hybrid forms are striking and colourful. Amongst the most popular are 'Snow Queen' white, 'Ottawa' deep violet and 'Perry's Blue'. 'Perry's Pygmy' is a dwarf blue-flowered form. Increased by division after flowering. 30–75 cm (1–2½ ft).

Fig. 24 Constructing an independent bog garden.

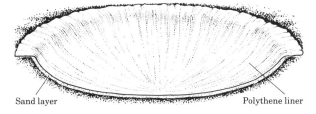

Sand layer · Polythene liner

(a) A PVC or polythene liner used in a sand-lined excavation.

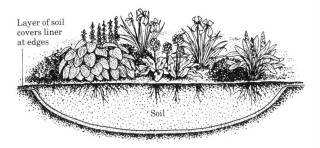

Layer of soil covers liner at edges · Soil

(b) Fill with a moisture-retentive soil and plant.

71

An informal planting using primulas and rushes provides a successful transition from bog garden to pool.

Lythrum salicaria (purple loosestrife). Bushy stems up to 1.2 m (4 ft) high carry slender spikes of deep rose-purple blooms. Named varieties include 'The Beacon', 'Lady Sackville' and 'Robert' which range in colour from purple, through rose-pink to pink. Common purple loosestrife is increased from seed, cultivars by division during early spring.

Mimulus hybrids (musk). The majority of *Mimulus* require boggy conditions. Those best suited to the garden water feature are largely derived from *M. luteus* and *M. tigrinus*. Amongst the finest are the pastel-coloured 'Monarch Strain', 'Queen's Prize' and the bright red 'Bonfire'. All the popular cultivars flower from midsummer until autumn. Easily raised from a spring sowing of seed. 15–45 cm (6 in–1½ ft).

Primula species. A large number of species and hybrids flourish in the damp of the bog garden. The following provide a continuity of colour. All can be raised successfully from seed either immediately after they ripen or during early spring.
  P. aurantiaca. One of the first candelabra primulas to flower. Tiers of bright orange blossoms in late spring. 75 cm (2½ ft).
  P. bulleyana. A candelabra species with orange-yellow flowers during mid-summer. 75 cm (2½ ft).
  P. denticulata (drumstick primula). Spring-flowering with rounded heads of blue or lilac flowers on short stout stems. 30 cm (12 in).
  P. florindae (Himalayan cowslip). Appears rather like a cowslip, but many times larger, reaching a height of 90 cm (3 ft) under favourable conditions. Late summer flowering.
  P. japonica. Crimson blossoms in dense tiered whorls above bright green cabbagy leaves during mid-summer. Cultivars like 'Miller's Crimson' and 'Postford White' are excellent. 60 cm (2 ft).
  P. rosea. One of the earliest and tiniest primulas for the bog garden. Brilliant rose-pink blossoms smother the ground-hugging foliage during early spring. 15 cm (6 in).

Trollius europaeus (globe flower). A bold yellow buttercup-like plant which flowers during spring. There are some excellent named varieties available. These include the soft yellow 'Canary Bird', intense orange 'Fire Globe' and 'Orange Princess'. Increased by division during the dormant period 60–90 cm (2–3 ft).

A bog garden planted
tastefully with primulas,
hostas and other moisture-
loving plants provides a
pleasing addition to the
pool.

· 5 ·
Fish and Other Livestock

As soon as planting is complete most gardeners have the urge to introduce fish. This should be resisted for several weeks as the plants take this amount of time to settle down and root sufficiently so that they are not disturbed by fish activity.

Any pool that is well planted is ideal for fish. Submerged plants are a fine spawning ground and also provide cover and a little green food. Deep water aquatics and floating plants give shade which is invaluable during the heat of a summer day. There are no particular specialized requirements for popular pond fish. Provided the recommended stocking rate is not exceeded, they will thrive under very modest circumstances.

Stocking rate
The most satisfactory stocking rate for decorative fish is 5 cm (2 in) of fish to every 0.093 sq m (1 sq ft) of surface area, excluding that occupied by the marginal plants. This rate of stocking allows for growth and development as well as encouraging natural breeding.

The calculation of the length of fish in this practical formula is based upon the total length including the tail. A pool where a total length of 90 cm (3 ft) is permitted, can have a fish population that may consist of three fish each 30 cm (12 in) long or twelve fish each 8 cm (3 in) long, or any combination of this that results in a total of 90 cm (3 ft). A number of fish fanciers stock more heavily than this, but an absolute maximum is 15 cm (6 in) of fish for every 0.093 sq m (1 sq ft) of surface area, unless a filtration system is envisaged.

Stocking with fish
Newly planted aquatics are extremely vulnerable to disturbance. Even quite small fish will poke around among the plants and retard their growth. A generous layer of pea shingle covering the compost in the containers will not always prevent this problem.

If the pool is to be a real success visually, then a well balanced mixture of fish is desirable. It is best to visit a specialist retailer or water garden nursery and look at the diversity available. Most suppliers of cold-water fish keep them in large aquariums, pre-formed pools or tanks that have no plant life but which are supplied with oxygen from an air line connected to a simple air pump. This provides an unimpeded view of what is available. Despite appearing rather clinical, these conditions are perfectly acceptable.

Choosing where to purchase fish from is almost as important as the number and variety of fish that you select. Always buy from a retailer who offers fish in tanks which are aerated from an air line. In an ideal situation the water in which the fish are swimming will be of a warm amber hue.

One of the best indications that a fish is in good health is the condition and stance of its fins. A stout upright dorsal fin and well-expanded ventral fins are indications that a fish is healthy. This can be confirmed also if the eyes are clear and bright. Fish with cloudy eyes should be avoided.

DECORATIVE POND FISH

Goldfish (Fig. 25)

The common goldfish is the best-loved ornamental fish for the garden pool. It comes in an array of colours, shapes and sizes unsurpassed in any other group of fish. The goldfish of the goldfish bowl is the same as that of the garden pond, although some gardeners express surprise that this should be so.

A goldfish in a bowl can live for many years and remains the same size as when first introduced. The goldfish seen in ponds are often large and in colours other than orange or red. The reason for the discrepancy in size is that a fish confined to a bowl will adapt to its surroundings and its growth will be arrested, whereas one that is at liberty in a garden pool will grow unimpeded. If a goldfish that has been confined to a bowl for several years is released into a pool, then it too will grow quickly.

Goldfish are very hardy, although if you are thinking of placing those from a bowl or aquarium into the pool it would be prudent to wait until late spring or early summer before doing so. Hardiness is largely the result of the fish gradually becoming accustomed to lower temperatures. During the winter there are few worries for the pool owner who has introduced ordinary goldfish to his water garden provided they have been put into the pool during the warm summer months. As autumn approaches their metabolism slows down and by winter they become more or less torpid, rather like a dormant tree.

● *Common goldfish* are brightly coloured fish varying from white through pink and yellow to orange and red, often with black markings. With many fish these black markings are temporary, being the remnants of the colour changing process from bronze when juvenile to golden as an adult. In a few cases they are permanent.

● *Comet-tail* is a very hardy long-tailed variety which comes in the same range of colours as the common kind. The tails are almost as long as the body and are graceful and flowing.

● *Fantail* is a rather chunky, rounded goldfish of great charm. The body is almost spherical, although retaining the characteristics of the common goldfish. The other variation is the fan-like tail which it carries in an almost horizontal fashion behind it. There are also versions of red or orange fantail goldfish with bulbous eyes. These are referred to affectionately as 'telescopes' and known in the aquatics' trade as either red telescopes or red and white telescopes.

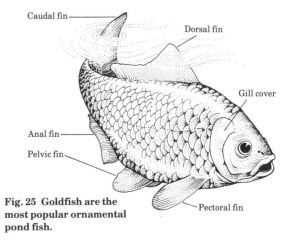

Fig. 25 Goldfish are the most popular ornamental pond fish.

Caudal fin — Dorsal fin — Gill cover — Anal fin — Pelvic fin — Pectoral fin

Whatever configuration the fantail has, it is vulnerable to both predators and water temperature change in the outdoor pool. With its rather cumbersome tail, it is slow moving and therefore easy prey for herons. Its developed and constricted body also leaves it more open to swim bladder problems.

Providing it is understood that fantails do not have quite the same resilience as ordinary goldfish, there is no reason why they should not be confidently introduced to a pool. Many pool owners have enjoyed years of pleasure from these remarkable fish.

Shubunkin

● *Common shubunkin* has the same general appearance as the common goldfish, although it rarely attains such a large size. Under favourable conditions a fish of 15–23 cm (6–9 in) is quite normal; anything larger than this is rather unusual. The common shubunkin is available in a wide range of colours and colour combinations, excluding green. Amongst commercial stocks the majority are red, white and yellow, often on a blue or grey ground and with a sprinkling of black spots or patches.

● *Calico comet* is a comet-longtailed version of the shubunkin, usually a bluish or grey colour splashed with red, orange, yellow and speckled with black spots. The tail is long, flowing and almost equal to the length of the body.

● *Calico fantail* is the fantail version of the shubunkin. A similar colour combination to that of the calico comet, but with a rounded dumpy body and a spreading tail. It is a questionable proposition for the garden pool, as its conformation and ungainly swimming technique render it vulnerable to environmental extremes and predators. Well worth a risk, provided you are aware that it is not as resilient as the common or comet-tailed varieties.

Carp

A group of fish with great diversity of size, shape and colour. Until recent years the carp that were available to us were perhaps rather dull. The advent of the Japanese Nishikigoi or Koi has changed all this, so much so that in many cases gardeners who start off by creating a balanced water garden end up as Koi fanciers. When this happens water gardening as we know it ceases and fish keeping takes over. Plants are removed, filters installed and a whole new hobby comes into being.

For the average garden pool of less than 3 m by 2.4 m (10 ft by 8 ft) it is not prudent to have more than two or three carp of any kind. They are boisterous fish and when present in quantity can cause problems by uprooting the plants and disturbing the soil in the baskets. They also yield a considerable amount of detritus which in turn provides nutrients for green water-discolouring algae. Having said that, most pools can tolerate the antics of two or three carp and they do provide much additional interest.

▶ Koi carp are amongst the most popular fish for the garden pool, although in large numbers they may damage the plants.

· FISH PESTS AND DISEASES ·		
Name	Description	Control
Anchor worm	A small white tube-like crustacean which embeds itself in the flesh of the fish.	Use a modern aquatic parasitic cure.
Fish louse	Small, almost transparent scale-like creature which infests fish, especially around the gills.	Use a modern aquatic parasite cure followed by a dip in malachite green to reduce the risk of fungal infection.
Fungus	White cottonwool-like growth attached to any part of the fish, but more usually the head, gills or tail.	Dip in a proprietary fungus cure.
Gill flukes	Invisible to the naked eye, but causes the fish to swim vigorously, periodically rushing to the surface of the water to gasp for air.	Parasite cures have some effect, but most afflicted fish are best destroyed.*
Slime and skin diseases	Afflicted fish are distressed and swim around irrationally. They have a bluish-white slime deposit which appears to be a combination of body slime and parasites.	Parasitic cures have some effect, but fish often have to be destroyed.*
White spot disease	White spots appear all over the body, head and tail; afflicted fish look listless.	Proprietary white spot cures are very effective; very small fish are rarely successfully treated.

* The most humane and quickest way to kill a fish is to wrap it in a small cloth and throw it onto a stone path.

● *Bronze carp* It may be a slight inaccuracy to include these here for they are really goldfish. However, the carp and goldfish are members of the same family and most gardeners classify these as carp. Of irregular occurrence at the fish retailers, these are nothing more than uncoloured goldfish. Young goldfish that are conceived in a low water temperature change colour slowly and appear as 'bronze' carp. Such fish are graded out of coloured goldfish by the breeders and marketed periodically. They are cheap and cheerful fish which often eventually change to red goldfish. Sometimes they are goldfish, in which the bronze colour is dominant. In this case, although you have no way of telling, they could introduce this undesirable trait to young fish if they interbreed with conventionally coloured goldfish.

● *Common carp* is a bronze or coppery coloured fish with a deep body, narrow head and four barbels. It should be avoided in the small pool as it is difficult to see in the bronze-amber waters and, in addition, tends to be rather boisterous.

● *Higoi carp* is the Chinese red carp, believed to be a variation of the common carp, but with a salmon or orange-pink body. A most attractive fish with a depressed head and distinctive barbels. This fish, like the Koi carp, grows rapidly and it is unwise to introduce more than two or three of them into the garden pond at the same time.

● *Koi carp* is the most startling of the carp family. The body shape is mostly like that of the Higoi, but the barbels are often smaller or absent. Some varieties have a metallic appearance, while others have scales that have a flat matt finish. There are all colours and combination of colours available in Koi.

Orfe and rudd (Fig. 26)
As a complement to brightly coloured goldfish and Koi carp there are a number of more modest fish species which can make an important contribution to the garden pool, yet co-exist quite happily with the other inhabitants. Not only that, by choosing outside the range of goldfish, carp and scavenging fish it is possible to introduce species like orfe, which occupy a totally different zone of the water. Both golden and silver orfe are surface swimmers, rarely venturing below the top 15 cm (6 in) of the water and enjoying the spray of fountain or waterfall. They also like leaping for flies which hover above the surface of the water.

● *Orfe* especially in its golden form, is a must for any pool. Swimming close to the surface of the water it is a constant source of interest and amusement as it darts about, periodically leaping into the air for gnats which dance just above the water. Their constant comings and goings add life to a pool, particularly the highly visible golden orfe which looks rather like a well grown carrot.

A slender fish, it is of an orange-pink colour often with dark or black blotches on and around the head. Small fish should initially be introduced to the pool as larger specimens do not travel well owing to their high oxygen requirement. This is no disadvantage, for golden orfe are amongst the fastest growing fish – a 5 cm (2 in) fish in the spring being quite 15 cm (6 in) by the autumn, ultimately attaining a length of between 30–45 cm (1–1½ ft).

The silver orfe or ide is a similar proposition that is not so attractive. Its body shape is long and slender like that of its golden cousin, but it is a plain silver colour with no hint of dark markings around the head. Sleek and elegant it behaves in a similar way, swimming close to the water

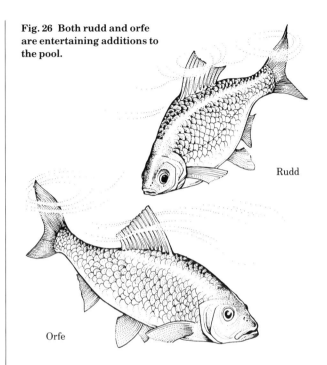

Fig. 26 Both rudd and orfe are entertaining additions to the pool.

Rudd

Orfe

surface and often plucking unwary insects from the air.

Neither the silver nor golden orfe breed readily in the small garden pool, but in large bodies of water in warm summers a brood of fry is quite likely.

● *Rudd* The common rudd is not often available to the pool owner, but both silver and golden variations are frequently offered.

The silver rudd has a metallic appearance and distinctive red fins, while its golden cousin is more coppery. Of the same general aspect as the goldfish, but of much more subdued colouration, both the golden and silver rudd are pleasing occupants of the garden pool, breeding freely where space allows and there is an abundance of underwater foliage.

79

SCAVENGING FISH

Most water gardeners believe that their pool must have a complement of scavenging fish if it is to function properly. This is a myth. Scavenging fish are invaluable for keeping the pool free from uneaten goldfish food which may decay and cause pollution as well as clearing up undesirable aquatic insect life like caddis fly and mosquito larvae. The idea that scavengers might clean the water, sucking up all manner of accumulated debris like an animated vacuum cleaner is sadly misconceived.

Scavenging fish are carnivorous. In a well ordered pool where there is no excess of fish food falling to the bottom they are largely unnecessary, although the majority of water gardeners prefer to have one or two scavenging fish present for peace of mind.

Green tench

The green tench is the most common scavenging fish for the garden pool. A short, broad olive-green or grey fish with an elegant body and narrow tapering head. Like all scavengers, once introduced to the pool it is rarely seen, lurking on the bottom amongst submerged plants and feeding upon gnat larvae and other aquatic insect life.

Although they rarely breed in the garden pool, male and female fish are readily distinguished, the male having a large central fin which extends to the rear orifice, the female with a weaker finnage in all respects.

In addition to the common green tench there is a golden variety. This is very hardy and beautiful, but provides little pleasure in the bottom of the pool. It is best as an inhabitant of the large cold-water aquarium.

▶ The great pond snail grazes on aquatic plants. It can be captured by floating fresh lettuce leaves on the pool.

FRESHWATER SNAILS AND MUSSELS

In addition to the fish a number of crustaceans can be benefically introduced to the garden pool. While not critical in creating and maintaining a balanced environment, they certainly contribute to the pool's well-being. A number of snails graze upon algae and rotting vegetation, providing a useful cleaning and scavenging function. They are particularly useful for removing unsightly algae such as the common mermaid's hair which clings to the walls of the pool and colonizes planting baskets and submerged plants.

Snails are also very useful indicators of excessively acid water, their shells becoming thin and pitted. When water conditions are alkaline the shells take on a smooth lustrous appearance.

Fresh water mussels contribute to keeping the pool water algae-free, sucking in green water, then releasing it having retained the offending suspended algae. As they are particular about their environment it is unwise to move mussels about more than necessary. Once settled in a pool they should remain undisturbed.

Snails

There are a number of different species of snail which may appear in a garden pool. Many of them will arrive naturally either as eggs stuck to the feet of bathing birds, or on purchased aquatic plants. While it cannot be denied that all will to some extent feed upon algae, it is fact that the majority much prefer to graze on desirable water plants. Any snails that have pointed shells must be treated with suspicion. Certainly none with a tail or spiralled shell should be deliberately introduced to the pool. It is only the flat disc-like species such as the ramshorn snail that are solely algae-eaters.

Mussels

The swan mussel is the most commonly available; this is a large mussel, up to 15 cm (6 in) long, with a dull brownish-green oval shell and white fleshy body. It is an efficient filter, but a complement rather than a substitute in the battle to control green water. Both this and the painter's mussel are only successful in an established pool with a layer of debris on the floor. In clear water in a new pool they rarely survive.

FROGS, TOADS AND NEWTS

Small amphibians such as frogs, toads and news are among the water gardener's best friends. They each play their part in helping to keep the pool environment healthy and they also add greatly to its interest.

Common frog

These breed during spring and early summer, when both males and females enter the water. Once fertilization has been completed, the tiny tadpoles which develop from the jelly-like spawn for a time feed on algal growth.

Frogs will find their own way to garden ponds, which are becoming one of their most important habitats.

Common toad

With their tough, brownish, warty skin and ungainly walk, toads are not generally as appealing as frogs. However they are a wonderful asset to any pond area as they feed almost exclusively on slugs, snails and other garden pests.

Newts

There are several kinds of newts which at different stages in their life cycle live in water or in the surrounding damp areas where they feed on all kinds of insects.

Managing the Water Garden

While the properly established water garden requires little labour intensive management, you should always be alert to impending problems. Although they happen rarely, the impact can be quite rapid and devastating. Careful observation plays dividends, while enjoyment can be much enhanced by breeding a few fish or increasing your stock of plants.

Algae control
Aquatic algae occurs in numerous forms, but from the pond owner's point of view these can be divided into free-floating and filamentous. The free-floating kinds comprise several hundred species which swarm in great masses and give water the appearance of pea soup. The filamentous kinds on the other hand appear as free-floating spirogyra or silkweed which can be dragged from the pool by the handful, or else in thick fibrous mats known commonly as blanket or flannel weed. Other filamentous species cling to plants and baskets and often coat the walls of the pool as well.

There is no easy method of curing the various algal problems that beset pool owners. The best permanent solution is achieved by a natural ecological balance, although this is often difficult to attain in a very small pool. In a naturally balanced water garden the higher plants provide competition for mineral salts and create shade in the water beneath. Chemical controls are only temporary solutions, although they can be very useful before a pool is well established, when the higher plants are not fully effective. Elimination of water-discolouring algae at this stage allows more light to enter the water and provides the submerged plants with a much better start.

Free-floating algae can be easily controlled by the use of an algaecide based upon potassium permanganate. Treatment must be on a dull day when the water is not too warm, or else the pool will turn a thick cloudy yellow and have to be emptied. On no account should potassium permanganate crystals be used on their own. The margin for error is very small, especially when fish are present. An excessive dose may also adversely affect some of the higher plants.

Filamentous algae can be controlled with proprietary algaecides based upon a carefully formulated copper sulphate solution. After treatment all the dead algae must be removed to prevent deoxygenation of the water.

Dirty water
If the pool turns dirty and muddy there is no cure other than cleaning the pool out completely. The result of soil deposits, once these have escaped from the containers every passing fish will cause the particles to swirl in the water rather like a cloud of brown smoke.

Soil has usually been removed from the planting baskets by the activities of fish which are nosing around in search of the grubs of aquatic insect life. Gnat larvae often populate planting containers and are considered to be a great delicacy by fish. If the planting baskets have a generous covering of pea shingle the larvae can be removed without disturbing the soil; when there is only a sparse covering of gravel, or none

· AQUATIC PLANT PESTS ·		
Name	*Description*	*Control*
Brown china mark moth	Cuts and shreds foliage of aquatic plants; makes a shelter for itself out of pieces of folded-over leaves.	Handpicking for small infestations; widespread damage can only be contained by complete defoliation.
Caddis fly	Many species, all of which feed upon the foliage of aquatic plants; they stick pieces of plant together to create small shelters in which they live.	Chemical control is impossible as the pests are hidden away safely in their protective shelters; fish are the best control.
False leaf-mining midge	Tiny larvae which create a narrow tracery of lines over the surface of the leaves which turn brown and decay.	A jet of clear water applied to the foliage will wash the larvae into the water where the fish can clear them up.
Snails	Pointed shelled snails all attack aquatic plants, chewing large pieces out of them.	There is no chemical control; float a fresh lettuce leaf on the surface of the water overnight and the snails will congregate beneath; they can then be removed and destroyed.

at all, the pool is likely to be muddy for much of the summer.

Black or blue water, usually accompanied by a foul smell, is an indication that something unpleasant is decomposing in the water. It may be freshwater mussel, fish or perhaps a small mammal like a hedgehog that has taken a tumble into the pool and drowned. Cleaning the pool out entirely is the only course of action.

Dealing with predators
There are several predators which cause problems for the inhabitants of the pool. Surprisingly the commonest is likely to be the heron, even in the suburban garden of large conurbations. Heron netting which covers the entire pool is available from some garden centres and although it keeps the heron out, it makes for a very messy pool and is not conducive to satisfactory plant growth, the young shoots having to push quite unnaturally through the netting. As the heron walks into the water to fish it is possible to create an equally successful defence which is not so offensive to the eye.

Take a number of short pieces of cane, up to 15 cm (6 in) long and push them into the ground at intervals of about 1.5 m (5 ft) around the pool, especially where the poolside is open to the surrounding ground. Attach to these a single strong strand of black garden cotton or fishing line. When the heron walks towards the water its legs come in contact with the thread and it will depart.

Cats can also be tiresome. They are not as great a problem as many pool owners believe, but a persistent cat can be very trying. In order to prevent fishing from the poolside, plant as much of the marginal area of the pool with a strong growing aquatic as possible. Where the pool meets the surrounding ground it is wise to pave

the edge, ensuring that the paving has a generous overhang. This enables fish swimming towards the side to have a refuge beneath which they can escape the grasping paw of the cat.

INCREASING YOUR OWN PLANTS

Aquatic plants are readily propagated by the home gardener. Some of the techniques differ slightly from those used for ordinary land plants, but the principles are broadly speaking the same.

Water-lilies from eyes (Fig. 27)

Water-lilies are all increased by division or from eyes. The only exception is *Nymphaea pygmaea* 'Alba' which has to be raised from seed. Both dividing water-lilies and growing them from eyes are allied, for the main branch-like divisions that are removed when an established water-lily is lifted and divided are the mature growths produced by eyes. It is just that reproducing plants this way is not the most economical use of the available propagation material.

All mature water-lilies produce eyes with varying frequency along their scrambling rootstocks. These eyes are rather like those of a potato, except that in most cases they will have tiny shoots on them that will appear like the juvenile growth of a water-lily. If detached from the rootstock that is what they will become, while if allowed to remain where they are, most will stay in a semi-dormant state. A few break into growth and produce the branch-like rootstocks that are familiar when established water-lilies are lifted from the pool.

◀ **Excess submerged aquatic plant growth must be carefully controlled so that a natural balance is maintained in the pool.**

▶ **A saucepan of boiling water to melt through the ice is the safest way of enabling noxious gases to escape.**

▲ Herons are said to be deterred from fishing in your pond if you introduce a likeness.

Fig. 27 Propagating water-lilies from eyes.

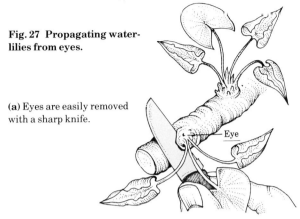

(a) Eyes are easily removed with a sharp knife.

Eye

(b) Potted eyes soon develop their own roots.

Water level above the eyes

The removal of water-lily eyes involves taking a sharp knife and digging them out of the flesh of the rootstock.

The adult water-lily is returned to the pool and the eyes potted individually in small pots of heavy garden soil or a properly formulated aquatic planting compost – that produced for potting full grown plants is perfectly adequate. The pots should be stood in an aquarium or shallow tray of water, ideally with the protection of a greenhouse. The water level should be no more than 2.5 cm (1 in) above the surface of the pots.

As the eyes produce shoots the water level should be gradually raised and they should be potted on progressively into larger pots until of a suitable size for planting out in the pool.

Water-lilies from seed

Of the hardy water-lilies only *N. pygmaea* 'Alba' can be raised from seed and produce uniform progeny that are true to type.

Water-lily seed is easily raised if sown in good quality, finely sieved garden soil or commercial aquatic planting compost.

Spread the jelly-like material containing the seeds across the surface of the compost. This is best done with a pair of tweezers. Cover with a thin layer of compost and stand the pot or pans in a bowl or aquarium of water. The water should barely cover the surface of the pots and the container must then be placed in a warm room or greenhouse with plenty of light, but not direct sunshine.

Seed raising

A number of aquatic plants can be raised annually from seed if desired. Some, like the water forget-me-not and musk, are very easily raised and often make a much better show if scrapped each year and replaced with fresh plants. Others are rather slow to increase by other means, so if a group of one type of plant is required seed may be the most satisfactory and economical way forward.

The sowing of seed of aquatic plants follows along the same lines as for terrestrial plants.

Sow the seed on the surface of the compost in the usual fashion, distributing the seed as evenly as possible. Cover lightly with compost or silver sand and water well. Take the pots and pans and place in a shallow container with the water level just beneath the surface of the compost. If it rises above the surface there is a chance that the seed may float away, particularly fine seed which is scarcely covered with compost. When growing away lustily they can be pricked out in the same way as any other garden plants.

Division

In the normal course of pool maintenance it becomes necessary to lift and divide plants periodicallly. Propagation can be effected at this time, causing minimal disturbance to the pool. Many marginal aquatics divide readily, much in the same way as herbaceous plants, although rarely is it necessary to take a spade or a fork to them if division has been a regular and timely occurrence.

Cuttings

Several aquatic plants can be increased from short stem cuttings of non-flowering growth.

Once growth commences in the spring take short cuttings of stem no more than 5 cm (2 in) long. Make the cut at a leaf joint, for it is here that the greatest cellular activity takes place and from where the cuttings are likely to root most successfully. Aquatic plants do not require the sophisticated growing media that other plants demand when rooting cuttings. A tray of mud that is placed just beneath the surface of the water is ideal. The cuttings are just pushed into this and root very quickly. (Fig. 28)

BREEDING FISH

The breeding season for popular ornamental cold water fish extends from late spring until late summer and is believed to be activated by the intensity of light and temperature of the water. Nobody has defined exactly what these criteria are, but bright summer sunshine for two or three days usually stirs sexually mature fish into fervent activity. This always assumes that the fish are in good health and that there is adequate plant cover for the deposition of spawn. In barren conditions a female fish that is in breeding condition will often reabsorb her spawn if the surroundings are not considered to be conducive to its survival.

When fish start breeding in a garden pool of their own accord it is an indication that the pool is in balance. For the newcomer to pond-keeping it can be a time of concern, for swimming in the water are masses of tiny young fish which are being preyed upon each day, often by their parents. The instinct to save every individual is strong, but should be resisted, for it is natural for the smaller and weaker individuals to perish and provide nourishment for the other inhabitants of the pool. Sufficient fry usually escape to grow into mature fish and make up any deficiencies in numbers.

Fig. 28 Aquatic plants such as *Mimulus ringens* can be increased freely from short stem cuttings rooted in a tray of mud.

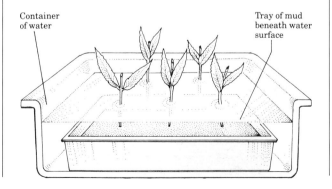

Container of water

Tray of mud beneath water surface

◄ Full of colour and interest, the summer pool requires little maintenance if properly stocked from the outset.

◄ The same pool in winter looks stark and lifeless, but even now it has a frosty beauty.

· 7 ·
The Water Gardener's Calendar

Apart from the depths of winter, the water garden keeps the gardener busy. Even then, if the weather turns really severe the water garden must be regularly monitored. Severe frost not only causes problems within the pool, but thick ice in a concrete pool can exert such a pressure that it causes fracturing of the structure. A rubber ball or piece of timber floated on the water from autumn onwards is a wise precaution. These are capable of absorbing tremendous pressure from expanding ice and can save the pool from damage.

Icing over does not threaten the existence of most aquatic plants or fish because of low temperature. It is the exclusion of gaseous exchange between the water body and the air which creates problems. Even small quantities of decomposing accumulated debris on the pool floor produces gases which are capable of asphyxiating fish if they are not permitted to escape into the air. A layer of ice across the pool prevents this, the gases building up in the gap between water surface and ice.

So winter is an important time, but not a particularly active one. It is the spring when everything happens, for it is then that most gardeners consider constructing a pool. Planting and stocking with fish follows quickly on its heels, for if by early summer everything can be in place, a reasonable show is assured for the first season. Aquatic plants and fish can be introduced from early spring until late summer, but the later this is done the less chance of creating an appealing picture, for aquatic plants are rapid growers which have to be cut back severely before planting.

Summer brings enormous enjoyment, for most of the plants are in flower and the fish are gliding happily amongst the water-lily pads. Growth is luxurious but conditions for exuberant growth are usually perfect for pests and diseases as well. Keep a constant look out for insect pests like water-lily aphids. Although impossible to spray with an insecticide when there are fish in the pool, a well aimed hosepipe will dislodge them and provide a feast for waiting fish.

Fish feeding using a variety of pond foods is not essential, but fun. By regularly feeding at one point in the pool it is possible to persuade the fish to attend there at the casting of your shadow or the sounds of your footfall. Providing that uneaten fish food is removed before it has an opportunity to sink to the floor of the pool, feeding the fish is a pleasurable and harmless occupation, even though in the well ordered pool there is likely to be sufficient natural food for all.

Autumn brings the tidying up phase and preparing both fish and plants for the winter. By the removal of decaying plant material and good general garden hygiene much can be done to break the life cycle of some of the water garden's most troublesome pests. Even though the plants are being tucked up for the winter the pool still has its charm, for now it is not so much a home to a glorious array of plants, but a reflective mirror in the middle of the garden.

SPRING

Pool preparation
- A garden pool can be constructed now if soil conditions are suitable.
- A waterfall or fountain can be installed.
- Aquatic plants can be safely planted in containers. Fish can be introduced to the pool as soon as new plantings have become established.

Maintenance
- Lift and divide water-lilies and other established aquatics and replant in fresh compost. This should be done every three or four years depending upon variety.
- Fertilize established aquatics using sachets of special water plant fertilizer pushed into the baskets next to the plants so that the fertilizer is released where it will be used and not into the water.
- Start to feed fish as soon as they are seen swimming about.

Pests and diseases
- Any water-lilies showing signs of root rot should be removed and the pool disinfected.
- Use a strong jet of water to dislodge water-lily aphids if they appear on the foliage of water-lilies and other succulent aquatic plants.

- Any fish that show signs of fungal growth must be netted from the pool and treated with a proprietary fish fungus cure before returning to the pool.

SUMMER

Pool preparation
- A garden pool can be constructed now.
- A waterfall or fountain can be installed.
- Aquatic plants can be introduced to the pool.
- Fish can be introduced to the pool as soon as the new plantings have become established.
- Pool repairs can be carried out.

Maintenance
- Lift and divide water-lilies and other established aquatics and replant in fresh compost. This should be done every three or four years depending upon variety.
- Fertilize established aquatics using sachets of special water plant fertilizer pushed into the baskets next to the plants so that the fertilizer will be released where it will be used and not into the water.
- Feed fish regularly. After 20 minutes remove any uneaten food from the pool with a net or else this may pollute the water. Pelleted fish foods float for longer than other kinds and are the easiest to use. Remove faded flower heads from aquatic plants to prevent them seeding. Apart from being an unnecessary drain on the plants' resources, it can result in unwanted seedlings appearing at random throughout the pool.
- Water-lilies can be propagated from eyes removed from their rootstocks and grown on in a small bowl or aquarium.
- Many marginal plants can be increased from short stem cuttings which are rooted in pots of mud.

- Aquatic plants that are to be raised from seed should be sown immediately the seed ripens.
- Treat any stubborn algal growths with a recommended algaecide.

Pests and diseases

- Any water-lilies showing signs of root rot should be removed and the pool disinfected.
- Use a strong jet of water to dislodge water-lily aphids if they appear on the foliage of water-lilies and other succulent plants.
- Handpick the larvae of china mark moths if they appear.
- Any fish that look listless must be isolated until the problem has been identified and treated. The two commonest diseases are white spot and fungus.

AUTUMN

Pool preparation

- A garden pool can be constructed now if soil conditions are suitable.
- A waterfall or fountain can be installed.

Maintenance

- As aquatic plants fade, cut them back in preparation for the winter. This also removes hiding places for hibernating pests. Do not cut marginal aquatic plant stems below the level of the water or else the plants may rot.
- Gather the turions or winter buds of floating aquatics like frogbit and place these in a bowl of water with a little soil on the bottom. These can then be advanced in growth in the spring. Remove the submersible pump and store inside for the winter.
- If you have a pool heater, attach this to the cable that carries the electrical supply to the pump.

- Net the pool for the period that leaves are falling from nearby trees to prevent the build-up of organic matter within the pool. Accumulated leaves decompose and produce toxic gases during the winter.
- Feed pond fish with high protein foods like ants eggs and dried flies in order to build up their energy reserves before the winter.

Pests and diseases

- Any water-lilies showing signs of root rot should be removed and the pool disinfected.
- Any fish that show signs of fungal growth must be netted from the pool and treated with a proprietary fish fungus cure before returning to the pond.

WINTER

Pool preparation

- A garden pool can be constructed now if soil conditions are suitable.
- A waterfall or fountain can be installed.

Maintenance

- Always ensure that during severe weather there is an area of open water in the pool. Use a pool heater or regularly melt a hole in the ice with a pan of boiling water placed on the surface, allowing it to melt through.
- Resist the temptation to feed fish, even if you see them swimming about. Any food placed in the water is likely to sink and cause pollution.

Pests and diseases

- Any water-lilies showing signs of root rot should be removed and the pool disinfected.
- Spray cherry and plum trees with a winter wash to kill the over-wintering eggs of water-lily aphids.

Appendix

SELECTED WATER GARDEN SPECIALISTS

U.K.

**Bennetts' Water Lily
and Fish Farm**
Chickerell
Weymouth
Dorset DT3 4AF

**Blagdon Water Garden
Centre Ltd**
Bath Road
Upper Langford
Avon BS18 7DN

Deanswood Plants
Potteries Lane
Littlethorpe Row
Ripon
North Yorkshire

Higher End Nursery
(D. J. Case)
Hale
Fordingbridge
Hampshire SP6 2RA

Honeysome Aquatic Nursery
The Row
Sutton, Nr. Ely
Cambridge CB6 2PF

Longstock Park Nursery
Stockbridge
Hampshire SO20 6EH

Maydencroft Aquatic Nurseries
Maydencroft Lane
Gosmore
Hitchin
Hertfordshire SG4 7QD

Stapeley Water Gardens Ltd
London Road
Stapeley
Nantwich
Cheshire CW5 7LH

Torbay Water Gardens
St Marychurch Road
Newton Abbot
Devon TQ12 4SE

The Water Garden Nursery
Highcroft
Moorend
Culmleigh
Devon EX18 7SG

Waveney Fish Farm
Park Road
Diss
Norfolk IP22 3AS

Wildwoods Water Garden Centre
Theobold Park Road
Crews Hill
Enfield
Middlesex EN2 9BP

Woodholme Nursery
(J. and F. Mimmack)
Stock
Essex

Wychwood Carp Farm
Farnham Road
Odiham
Basingstoke
Hampshire RG25 1HS

NORTH AMERICA

A Fleur D'Eau
G.P. 119 Route 237
Stanbridge
Quebec JOJ 2HO
Canada

Aloha Lilies
123 N. Regency Place
Tucson
Arizona
AZ 85711

**Aquatic Gardens and Koi
Company**
P.O. Box 57
Highway 537
Jobstown
New Jersey
NJ 08041

Bittersweet Hill Nursery
1274 Governor Bridge Road
Davidsonville
Maryland
MD 21035

C and C Aquatics
2635 Steel Drive
Colorado Springs
Colorado
CO 80907

C and S Water Gardens
1255 Oakhaven Drive
Roswell
Georgia
GA 30075

Florida Aquatic Nurseries
700 S. Flamingo Road
Fort Lauderdale
Florida
FL 33325

Gilberg Perennial Farm
2906 Ossenfort Road
Glencoe
Missouri
MO 63038

Lilypons Water Gardens
6800 Lilypons Road
Lilypons
Maryland
MD 21717–0010
and
839 FM 1489
Brookshire
Texas
TX 77423

Moore Water Gardens
Box 340
Port Stanley
Ontario NOL 2A0
Canada

Paradise Water Gardens
14 May Street
Whitman
Massachusets
MA 02382

Reimer Waterscapes
RR No. Box 34
Tillsonburg
Ontario
N4G 4H3
Canada

**Santa Barbara Water Gardens
and Landscapes**
P.O. Box 4353
Santa Barbara
California
CA 93140

Scherer and Sons
104 Waterside Road
Northport
New York
NY 11768

Slocum Water Gardens
1101 Cypress Gardens Boulevard
Winter Haven
Florida
FL 33880

Tilley's Nursery
111 E. Fairmont Street
Coopersburg
Pennsylvania
PA 18030

The Tranquil Water Lily
4761 Olive Street
San Diego
California
CA 92105

Valley View Farms
11035 York Road
Cockeysville
Maryland
MD 21030

Waterford Gardens
74 East Allendale Road
Saddle River
New Jersey
NJ 07458

Waterscapes
5520 Little River Circle
Gainesville
Georgia
GA 30506

W. Rolf Ltd
443 Paso Del Norte
Escondido
California
CA 92026

AUSTRALIA

Bau Farm Nursery
Brusner Highway
Wollongbar
Lismore
NSW 2480

Laurence Gedye
37–41 Elizabeth Street
Doncaster East
Victoria 3109

Johannes Harder
151 Arcadia Road
NSW 2159

Charles Winch
80 Arcadia Road
Arcadia
NSW 2159

Index

Page numbers in *italics* indicate an illustration or boxed table.

Algaecide, 82
Algal problems, 7, 67, 80–81, 91
Alisma plantago-aquatica, 63
Aponogeton distachyos, 62
Aquatic plants, 58–72, 74, 89–91
  containers, 58
  deep-water, 58, *59*, 60, *62*, *63*
  floating, 69, *70*, 74
  fountains and, 44
  marginal, 22, 26, 58, 63–64, *66*
  pests, 83
  planting, 38, 58–72
  propagation, 85–87
  ratio of, 58
  shade and, 7
  submerged for special purposes, *67*, 69
  sunlight and, 7
  see also individual names
Arrowhead, 66
Astilbe hybrids, 70
Azolla caroliniana, 69, *70*

Backfilling pool excavation, 24, 26
Blanket weed, 82
Bog arum, 63, *66*, 67
Bog bean, 63
Bog garden, 37, *38*, 39
  constructing an independent, *71*
  excavation, 39, *71*
  liner, 38–39
  plants, 70–72
  soil for, 38–39
Brooklime, 67
Bulrush, 66
Butomus umbellatus, 63

Calendar, water gardener's 89–91
Calla palustris, 63, *66*, 67
Caltha palustris, 63
Canadian pond weed, 69
Carp, 12, 76, 78–79
Ceratophyllum demersum, 67
Children, safety of, 13
Chinese water gardening, 11
Clay for puddled ponds
  choosing, 22
  bentonite, 22
  calcium, 22
  sodium, 22
Concrete pool, 27, *30–31*, 33, *34*, 35
  colourants, 27, 31
  constructing a, *31*
  excavating, 27, 30
  laying, 34
  sealing, 35
Constructing a water garden, 22–39
Containers, aquatic plant, 58
Creating a water garden, 7–19, 22–39
Crustaceans, 80
Cuttings, aquatic plant, *87*, 90

Design, water garden, 10–14
Division, aquatic plant, 85, 87
Drainage, need for, 8
Drumstick primula, 72

Eichornia crassipes, 69
Electrical cable, armoured, 15
Elodea canadensis, 69
Elodea crispa, 69
Erosion, soil, 54
Evaporation, water, 7

Fairy moss, 69, *70*
False goat's beard, 70
Filipendula ulmaria, 70

Fish, 42, 74–81, 89
  breeding, 87
  carp, 12, 76, 78–79
  cold-water, 74
  decorative pond, 74, *75*, 76
  feeding, 90–91
  goldfish, *75*, 76, 79
  green tench, 80
  Japanese carp *see* carp
  orfe, *79*
  pests, diseases, problems, 78, 82, 90
  rudd, *79*
  safe conditions for, 8
  scavenging, 80
  stocking, 74–75
  where to purchase, 74–75
Flannel weed, 82
Flooding problems, 10
Flowering rush, 63
Fountains, 13, 27, 42, 44, 46
  bubble, 13
  illuminated, 43, 46
  pebble, 51
  positioning, 44
  pump installation, 44, *46*
  spray, 42, *43*, 46
  types of, *43*, 47
  unit, basic, 46
Frogbit, *70*, 91
Frogs, 81
Frost pockets, 8

Gargoyles, decorative, 47–48
Globe flower, 72
Gnat larvae, 83
Golden club, 63
Goldfish, *75*, 76, 79
  selecting, 76
Gravel, fine and pea, 24
Green tench, 80

Hessian liners, 58, *59*
Higoi carp *see* Carp
Himalayan cowslip, 72
Hornwort, 67
Hosta, 71
Hottonia palustris, 69
Hydrocharis morsus-ranae, *70*

Iris, 7, 64, *66*
  bog-garden varieties, 71

Japanese water gardening, 11–12, 14

Koi carp *see* Carp

Lagarosiphon major, 69
Laydekeri hybrids *see Nymphaea*;
  water-lilies
Lighting
  colour changing, 57
  fountain, 43, 46, 57
  underwater, 57
  waterfall, 57
Liners
  artificial stream, 54
  bog garden, 38–39
  constructing a pool, *23*
  pool, 8, 14
  pre-lining fleece, 23
  types of pool, 24
  wildlife and, 39
Lutyens, Edwin, 11
Lythrum salicaria, 72

Managing the water garden, 82–87
Marking out a pool, 15–18
  circle, *18*
  oval, *18*
  right-angle, *15*

Marginal aquatic plants, 22, 26, 58,
  63–64, *66*, 90–1
Marsh marigold, 7, 63
Masks, decorative, 47–48
Meadow sweet, 70
Mentha aquatica, 64
Menyanthes trifoliata, 64
Mimulus hybrids, 72
Musk, 72, 86
Mussels, 80
Myosotis scorpioides, *64*
Myriophyllum spicatum, 69

Newts, 81
Nishikigoi *see* Carp
Nuphar lutea, 62, *63*
Nymphaea, 58, 59, 60, 62, 63
  hybrids, 63
Nymphoides peltata, 63

Orfe, *79*
Ornaments, 13–14, 27, *43*, 47–48
  see also Fountains
Orontium aquaticum, 63

Pea shingle, 74, 83
Pebble fountain, 51
Pickerel, 66
Plantain lily, 71
Plants and planting, 58–72
  submerged, *67*, 69
Polythene liner, 30, 71
Pond *see* pool
Pontederia cordata, *66*
Pool
  backfilling with excavated soil, 24,
    26
  concrete, 27, *30–31*, 33, *34*, 35
  design of a, 14
  excavation materials, 23–24, 26
  flexible, 26–27
  formal, *10*
  informal, *30*, 36
  liner, 8, 23–24, *23*, 39
  maintenance, 90–91
  membrane, polythene, 30
  natural earth, 22
  pests and diseases, 90

predators, 83, 85
pre-formed, 8, 19, 24, *26*, 26
preparations for a , 23–24, 27, 90–91
puddled, clay for, 22, 39
raised, *19*
reflections, 10–12, 27
shape of, *11*, 14, 15–18
shuttering, 30, 33, *34*
wetland surround, 39
wildlife, 12–13, 39
Potassium permanganate, 82
Predators, pool, 83, 85
Primula, 72
Problems
  algae, 7, 67, 80–82, 91
  dirty-water, 82–83
  drainage, 8
  erosion, 54
  fish pests and diseases, 78
  flooding, 10
  pests and diseases, 78, 89–91
  slime, 67
  soil saturation, 8
  soil spillage, 38–39
  water evaporation and loss, 7
  weeds, 67, 82
Propagation, aquatic plant, 85–87, 90
  seed, 86
  water-lilies from eyes, 85, *86*
  water-lilies from seeds, 86
Pumps
  modern water, 13, *14*
  submersible, 42, 44, *46*
Purple loosestrife, 72
PVA (polyvinyl acetate) adhesive, 36
PVC excavation liner, *71*
Pygmaea hybrids *see Nymphaea*;
  water-lilies

Reedmace, 66
Rills *see* Streams
Rudd, *79*

Safety, children's, 13
Sagittaria japonica, 66
Scavenging fish, 80
Scirpus hacustris, 66
Sealants, 35

Seed, aquatic plant, 86
Shade, aquatic plants and, 7
Shape, 10–11
    circular pool, *18*, *30*
    formal, *10*
    informal, *30*, 36
    oblong or square pool, 15
    oval pool, *18*
    see also Marking out a pool
Shubunkin, 76
Shuttering, pool, 30, 33, *34*
    curved, 34
    removing, 34
Sink water garden, 36–37
    coating mixture for, 36–37
Site
    preparing, 14
    raised, 18, *19*
    selecting a, 7–8
    sloping, 18
Snails, freshwater, 80–81
Soil, bog garden, 38–39
    erosion, 54
    saturation, 8
    spillage prevention, 38–39
Sparganium, 22
Spiked milfoil, 69
Stratiotes aloides, *70*
Streams, 51, 54
    artificial, 54–55
    excavating, 54, *55*
    pre-formed, 55, 57
Sunlight, aquatic plants and, 7

Temperature, pool, 7
Toads, 81
Trapa natans, 70
Trollius europaeus, 72
Tub water garden, *35*
    charring, 35
    lining a, 35
    plants for, 60
Typha, 22, 66

Veronica beccabunga, 67

Water
    dirty, 82–83

evaporation and loss, 7
garden specialists, selected, 92–93
moving, 13, 27, 42–57
plants *see* Aquatic plants and
    individual names
pumps, modern, 13
safety of children and, 13
still, 10–12, 27
table, 8
temperature, 7
see also Ponds, Streams and
    Waterfalls
Water chestnut, 70
Waterfalls, 43–44, 47–49, *50*, *51*
    installation, 50–51
    lighting, 57
Water forget-me-not, 64, 66, 86
Water fowl, 39
Water fringe, 63
Water hawthorn, 62
Water hyacinth, 69
Water-lilies, 11, 13, 26, 42–44, 58, *59*,
    60, *62*, *63*
    pests and diseases, 62
    planting depth, *59*
    propagation, 85, *86*
    root rot, 90–91
    top-dressing, 59
    varieties, 58, *59*, 60, *62*, *63*
Water mint, 64
Water plantain, 63
Water soldier, *70*
Water violet, 69
Weedkiller, 54
Wetland surround, 39
Wildlife, 12–13, 39, 54

Yellow pond-lily, 62, *63*